Experiencer 2

Two Worlds Collide

William J. Konkolesky

Foreword by

Mike Clelland

Detroit, MI

website: experiencer.me

ISBN 978-1-716-46432-4

Printed in the United States of America

Published by Lulu Enterprises, Inc.

860 Aviation Parkway, Suite 300

Morrisville, NC 27560

First Edition

Illustration credits:

Front and back cover design and illustration by Mike Clelland.

Illustration on page 23 by Jeff Westover.

All other illustrations by the author.

Photos by the author and family members.

PRAISE FOR *EXPERIENCER: RAISED IN TWO WORLDS* AND *EXPERIENCER 2: TWO WORLDS COLLIDE*

"In that wide world of books written about truly anomalous UFO phenomena, there exists a category written by, not about, UFO abductees and experiencers. One of the finest in my experience is William Konkolesky's first book, *Experiencer: Raised In Two Worlds*. It caught me completely off guard in how well written it was, how objective the author re-mains throughout his sometime hair-raising narrative, and how moving and compelling the story it told. Now Konkolesky's new book, *Experiencer 2: Two Worlds Collide*, hits the same mark if not more so. It held my complete attention from start to finish, and, to be blunt, simply ranks among the finest books ever by this select group of authors. A must addition to your UFO library and recommended without reservation."

Peter Robbins
Investigative writer, UFO researcher and bestselling author

"From the start, one thing I liked is Konkolesky makes no claim the visitors are extraterrestrial, acknowledging the possibility they could just as well be from some place "else"—a higher dimension, a different plane of existence, possibly even our own planet, as 'cryptoterrestrials.' While this theory is considered controversial in the often rigid field of ufology, Konkolesky stands by his argument, and I agree with him...The book is a quick-read, offering a straightforward description of the events and their impact on the author throughout his life."

Deirdre Lavery
Review of *Experiencer: Raised in Two Worlds* for the *Journal of Abduction Research*

"There have been several book dealing with the alien abduction phenomenon, but Experiencer: Raised in Two Worlds stands out for its un-complicated delivery. Too many alien contactees attempt to mystify, demonize or sanctify the phenomenon. Konkolesky simply tells it like it is."

David Twichell
Author of *Global Implications of the UFO Reality*

"Konkolesky is courageous to come forward and describe the various incidents that have taken place throughout his life. He delivers what could be considered traumatic experiences with a personable flavor and genuine respect for all aspects of an otherworldly phenomenon."

Tony Sivalelli
Author of *Ambassadors to the Stars*

THANK YOU

There are far too many people to name that I thank for support. My wife, family, friends, co-workers, and the many, many wonderful individuals I have met within the UFO and greater paranormal community have been absolutely amazing. Thank you all.

A very special thank you to Mike Clelland for penning the thoughtful foreword and providing the wonderful cover art to this book.

This book is dedicated to the rock band A House for their extraordinary album I Want Too Much that I considered the soundtrack of my tumultuous early twenties, the time-frame of my personal accounts included in this volume.

A NOTE ON CONTENT

This book is arranged into three parts. In the first, I provide an introduction to the material, while also giving some updates to content from my first book. The second part is my personal narrative of my UFO and con-tact experiences during the early 1990s. The third part is a deeper examination of the more unusual accounts from the second part, thus allowing the second part narrative a better flow. I also include a remembrance of the late Budd Hopkins and conclude with some poems.

In this book, I sometimes refer to the beings I've encountered as 'alien' or 'extraterrestrial.' There may be some details about their origin that makes these terms technically incorrect, but until we know with absolute certainty, these commonly used terms are useful in getting the point across.

RAISED IN TWO WORLDS CORRECTION

In my first book, I recount a story of playing in my backyard trees with my friend Chet when a strange mist containing a gray entity rolled in and passed through the yard. I was seven years old, and Chet was six.

Shortly after the book came out, my friend Adam from childhood, whom I'd played with on a nearly daily basis, just like I did with Chet, corrected me that it was him and not Chet who was present for the event. While he was six at the time, he still remembered the mist over thirty years later but didn't see the accompanying entity as I did. Thank you, Adam, for the confirmation and please pardon for forgetting it was actually you.

TABLE OF CONTENTS

FOREWORD

This book is one person's story. It's a remarkable journey of strangeness and courage, told with a disarming sincerity that left me both shaken and reassured.

The UFO phenomena encompasses a lot, and much of it is complex and conflicting. There are divergent reality tunnels that can drag an individual, whether an experiencer or researcher, to a place of extremes, making it easy to get lost in shadowy ideas of space gods or evil conspiracies. Bill avoids the sensational extremes of the subject, yet he's able to address the strangest aspects with a calm objectivity. As someone immersed in these studies I truly appreciate his balanced voice. Sadly, in this field, such a levelheaded outlook is rare.

I've had similar experiences, so I was not an objective reader. Turning each page meant seeing my own reflection in his story, as if a pinging bell steadily counted the similarities in our lives—not only the events, but the emotions and fears.

I also grew up in Michigan, and recognized much of Bill's character in his story. He personifies the iconic mid-westerner—humble, thoughtful, and steady. Knowing Bill and our shared roots, it was impossible not to be drawn into the humility of his voice. He is an ordinary person, telling an extraordinary story.

Despite the calm tenor of his writing, he bravely takes the reader into the intense mystical aspects of his experiences; the high-strangeness, the timeless silence, the psychic premonitions, the powerful synchronicities, the orchestrated events, the prophetic dreams, and the ongoing role the beings have played in his life.

I once asked Bill, "How would you be different if these things had never happened in your life?"

Without hesitation, he replied, "Without these experiences, I wouldn't recognize myself."

We are now living in a new chapter of history. In December of 2017 the New York Times ran two articles about UFOs, both written without any of the "giggle" factor that has tainted the subject. The reports covered sightings by Navy pilots, and a government program that investigated un-identified flying objects. The Times has continued publishing articles that seem to affirm the reality of UFOs. That such a venerable institution would address such a taboo subject marked a transformative moment in the history of the UFO phenomenon. No longer fodder for the tabloids, it was now front and center in a wide spectrum of news sources.

Yet all this reporting remained focused only on the "nuts and bolts" aspect of the mystery—things like witness testimony of craft in the sky, radar returns, and video analysis. For those who've had firsthand contact experiences, these are mere surface issues, the deeper mystery is a tangled web of bizarre and elusive experiences. The challenge is to confront the heartfelt accounts told by abductees.

A Navy pilot can give a credible description of something physical seen from a jet fighter. But how does a young man in the suburbs describe the disturbing memories of face-to-face contact with something so unknowable?

This book is an insight into the shadow realm ignored by mainstream re-porting. Mystifying events have invaded the lives of people like Bill, and so many others. He is not alone, and if you the reader have experienced anything similar, you are not alone either.

There is a surface story to the UFO contact experience. We all know the pop culture narrative of abductions on lonely roads, and creepy medical procedures aboard flying saucers. This is part of the overall story, true enough, but there is a lot more going on below the waterline. This is difficult stuff and it challenges our very definition of reality.

When experiencers talk among themselves, whether in the halls of a UFO conference or on a late night phone call, what gets shared by one is often confirmed by the other, and this can turn a fleeting memory into an unsettling reality. It might be an eerily similar description of a room or a being, but more often it's a recognition that they are each trying to describe something that is indescribable; an altered mood of such strangeness that it's entirely separate from normal reality. One will say to the other, "Yes, I understand!" Then they'll follow with their own version of the same distortion of time and space. I know, because I've had these powerful moments of connection with other experiencers—and I've had them with Bill too.

We are the insiders. We can express our fears and awe to each other, yet it's terribly difficult to describe this to those who don't share our experiences. There is an even deeper strangeness in what Bill has endured—events and relationships seem to have been carefully orchestrated by the UFO occupants, as if they hold the puppet strings of his life. This could come across as paranoid, yet it was addressed so plainly in the book, and I've felt the same strings tied to me. These experiences need to be shared, no matter how weird. Telling his story so openly gives a voice to those who are, for good reasons, unable to share their own.

This book is a private conversation between you and Bill, and a deeply personal insight into the subtleties and absurdities of a grand mystery. Perhaps, the ultimate mystery.

Mike Clelland, 2020

author of *The Messengers*

Part One

Introduction

Experiencer 2

INTRODUCTION

This volume is the second installment of my unusual but true personal experiences of extraterrestrial contact. The incidents in this book go beyond what is commonly reported about this phenomenon. What I mean by this is that I detail what may be a surprising aspect of what is happening to at least a sub-group of experiencers.

The alien contact phenomenon is often much more than an abduction scenario where individuals get yanked from their bed or car, perhaps once in a lifetime. More often, experiencers get taken several times over several years, and the beings sometimes take a surprisingly active and even guiding interest in experiencers' day to day existence. Most importantly, in these scenarios, the entities can be keenly interested in who experiencers date or marry, even going so far as to step in and play match-maker on occasion. Sometimes, this match-making can be obvious, but, in most situations, their little gray fingerprints are harder to detect and, to identify the subtle clues, one may need to closely examine an evidence trail that can span years.

In this account of six years of my life from age 19 to 25, some very harrowing and very strange things did indeed happen to me and, in-between those events, even much of my mundane life seemed to be tied to visitors from elsewhere and their mysterious plans.

There is little in this account that doesn't wrap itself into the central phenomena-focused narrative. I don't pad or fluff the story simply to wax nostalgic about my early years. Individuals generally aren't mentioned unless they have a part to play in the bigger picture.

I ask the reader to please be patient with what may at first appear to be filler, and hopefully note how one encounter, event, or individual perhaps ties in with some or all of the others in this book.

These six years of my life were a rich tapestry and a bumpy ride. And never boring.

To those whom I mention in this book, I wish you well in life, apart from whatever unpleasant situations may have briefly transpired between us decades ago.

All names herein are pseudonyms with the exception of anyone I give both a first and last name, my wife Becky, and my parents (who are obviously my parents). Some friends are listed simply as "friends" if they are not central characters in the stranger parts of this story. To those friends, thank you for being in my life and thank you for your understanding.

Locations are sometimes withheld or are approximations to safeguard witnesses and other individuals from an uninvited spotlight.

Specific dates are usually instead given as approximations due to the challenge of trying to pinpoint so many of them with exactitude from nearly thirty years ago.

The story begins in my boyhood home in Sterling Heights, summer of 1990, and picks up literally at the conclusion of my book *Experiencer: Raised in Two Worlds*. If you haven't yet read that, it's the best place to see the foundations of what happens within these pages. Thank you for reading.

I suspect response to this book will fall widely into two categories - those who may appreciate seeing the surprising links between the contact phenomenon and our humble human lives – and those who see anything personal about the experiencers themselves as self-indulgent ramblings (*"nobody cares about you – I'm just here for the alien stuff"*).

To those in the second camp, I get it. Just before writing my first book, I revisited several of the alien contact books that inspired me to release my story. One thing that I took away from doing this was I chose to bypass much of the extraneous personal detail that I found to be in some of these works that dragged on the narrative.

The result for the final version of my account was to put out a somewhat lean book of primarily the experiences themselves.

I produced this book with this same sense of caution, though, as the focus of this book is specifically the human condition in connection with the contact phenomenon, it unavoidably has some more "me" stuff in it.

However this book is ultimately received, like my first book, I wrote it as much for myself as I wrote it for public consumption. It is an honest confession of true-life events recorded for my personal reflection and I hope there is value in it for other readers. Also, I hope my fellow experiencers appreciate a new book on our related close encounters. I'm but one of many, very many, who has lived through a life of persistent contact with beings more than a little curious about us.

ENCOUNTERS WITH CONSCIOUSNESS

In my first book, I refer to how the abduction and out-of-body phenomena appear to have many parallels. How do you know if you find yourself unexpectedly floating out of bed and through a wall in the middle of the night whether this is alien abduction or astral travel?

It appears that the extraterrestrials may actually be utilizing astral travel to facilitate some of their contact. If an encounter doesn't require a physical examination, only intellectual interaction, why should they sweat finding a place to park the flying saucer and working out how to take someone without drawing attention, if they can just pull someone out-of-body? It not only makes perfect logistical sense to do this, but it fits with the descriptions of many experiencers' encounters.

Can they actually do this? I not only believe this is absolutely possible, but I'll take speculation one step further and postulate that at least some of these beings' natural state is one of pure consciousness.

For starters, as these beings are clearly more technologically advanced than us, even a few hundred years lead on us could prove to be an incalculable difference and it's possible that some of the visiting civilizations are thousands of years ahead of us – even millions can't be ruled out.

It is not out of the question that, at some point in scientific advancement, a species discovers how to plug consciousness in and out of a receptive physical form. This form could be biological, technological, or some sort of hybrid. The species potentially then evolves to exist primarily in a state of pure consciousness and, when they need to interact with physicality, they put consciousness into drone-like puppet entities that could very well include what we see as gray aliens.

When humans see the beings' true selves when we are out of body, they seem to look the same to us as they do in the physical. Perhaps this is because they understand that we would have a hard time comprehending their natural etheric form and, so, intentionally appear to us in the gray entity form. Perhaps instead we subjectively impose an appearance on them that matches our physical recognition.

As there is much speculation here, there are admittedly some loose ends to work out, but I would say that the consciousness hypothesis addresses many unanswered questions about the contact phenomenon, including specific things that have happened to me that I relate in this book.

It is likely that humans will one day also be experimenting with combinations of consciousness and matter, ourselves (if it isn't already occurring somewhere in a black budget project!).

Extraterrestrials must be closely watching humanity on our journey of milestone steps, and that could very well include someday our evolution of consciousness apart from form.

FAMILY FOLLOW-UP

In my first book, I shared some paranormal events that have happened to my family. Further events have occurred. In particular, my two brothers whose paranormal experiences I recounted in my first book have had more episodes than I told about in *Experiencer: Raised in Two Worlds*.

My brother Trevor, whom I'd previously mentioned has experiences within the categories of psychic, poltergeist, and apparition, is also one of those individuals who affect electricity.

One thing he does, usually inadvertently, is powering off streetlights, a common object of affectation for those with this ability.

An ironic and humorous example of this is when he used to work a maintenance position for the city of Warren, Michigan. One evening, he was asked to drive through a subdivision and report any streetlights that were out. Peculiarly, as he made his patrol, an astonishing number of the lights turned off as he drove under them, only to turn back on as he drove away! He began to drive down streets he'd already gone down just to see the phenomenon repeat itself. His co-worker in the vehicle was dumbfounded.

One evening, a girl he was dating openly doubted his ability to affect streetlights and he pointed out his apartment window to a random light at the entrance to his complex and said he could make it go out if they walked out to it. They did and it did.

Another time, Trevor was driving to our mother's house when he was stopped at a traffic light. He glanced over at a roadside transformer box and it instantly blew out, shooting sparks and smoking.

I will also never forget that when he was a teenager, he was up on the roof of our house as a big thunderstorm rolled in. He pressed himself under the awning of the second story of our tri-level home to get out of the rain and watch the storm. He was treated to a lightning bolt striking the electric pole in front of our house!

A relatively minor but still fascinating aspect of Trevor's electrical ability is that he sometimes gets a static charge when he hugs others.

As a related aside, after a UFO presentation that I delivered at a local library a few years ago, a woman from the audience approached me in tears, saying that she was going to college to be a radiation tech, but that she kept accidentally making the expensive equipment fry out due to her ability to affect electrical devices. She did not know what to do, as this was her chosen career path. I was at a loss for what to tell her.

Trevor's psychic abilities include the power of premonition. These predictions generally manifest as clear images in his mind during waking hours, primarily afternoons. Perhaps the most dramatic of his premonitions is that he twice foresaw major plane crashes several weeks before they occurred.

In the first instance, during the summer of 1987, he psychically saw a passenger plane crash that he felt would occur locally. On August 16, 1987, Northwest Airlines Flight 255 crashed after takeoff onto nearby Interstate-94. All but one of the 149 passengers died, along with all six crew members and two drivers on the expressway.

More recently, in the summer of 2011, he saw a plane crash that he knew would involve hockey players. On September 7, 2011, a Russian charter flight, Yak-Service Flight 9633, crashed near the city of Yaroslavl, killing all but one of the 45 hockey players, their coaching staff, and the flight crew on board.

Curious perhaps that a handful of high-profile plane crashes over the years didn't drop onto Trevor's psychic radar if the Russian one did. Psychic powers can apparently be pretty random.

Some psychic messages that Trevor receives on others involve mundane situations (I suppose much like my knowing what my high school buddy was having for lunch, as mentioned in my first book). One time, Trevor was visiting his cardiologist and got an impression of her and her husband watching her daughter play tennis. Needing a distraction from boredom at his appointment, Trevor decided to tell her of his vision to gauge her reaction. She was open to hearing what he saw. He then went into great detail about what everyone looked like and was wearing, as well as the location of and weather during the tennis match. She became quite flustered and asked him if he was stalking her. For obvious reasons, as often has Trevor has these psychic visions, he generally keeps them to himself.

In two instances, he has had sobering visions of himself.

In one of his visions, he was a German soldier in Europe during WWII, watching someone from his unit being gunned down by the British. He feels quite certain that this vivid observation is an authentic memory from a past life.

In another vision, it is the future of his current life and he is in poor health as my brother Jerome visits him in the hospital.

The other brother of mine with a paranormal history, whom I spoke much of in *Raised in Two Worlds*, is John. There are two unusual accounts of him while he was driving that are worth recounting.

In one, about twenty years ago, he was by himself in his car, pulling out of a parking lot after shopping when he felt something grip his throat and yank him back as if someone was in the backseat choking him. He slammed on the brakes as a speeding car on the busy street in front of him unexpectedly switched lanes into the lane he was about to enter. The pressure on his neck then instantly disappeared and he double-checked to verify that there was no one in the vehicle with him. He believes that what occurred was some sort of guardian angel intervention to keep him from an accident.

In another episode, John and his teen daughter Rose (now an adult who now also experiences poltergeist activity!) had an unusual event happen to them, late at night, the summer of 2004, in a semi-rural area of southeast Michigan.

At just after 1am, on the morning of Aug. 27, 2004, John was driving from Imlay City, MI, to his home in Leonard with 14-year-old Rose in the passenger seat. He had picked her up from a visit to Rose's mother.

Suddenly, something very peculiar occurred. They instantly found themselves more than 6 miles away, heading in a different direction, on a road they didn't readily recognize, still traveling at the same rate of speed.

At the onset of their experience, the two of them were southbound on S. Lake Pleasant Road, just 15 minutes from their home, discussing the start of Rose's upcoming school year. John specifically recalls the time 1:09 AM on the dashboard clock, and the thought that they would easily be home before 1:30 AM on this very familiar route.

Then, suddenly, the road ahead suddenly "fogged" and then "pixilated" back into clarity. In an instant, John and Rose had both suddenly stopped their animated discussion as though they had actually completed it sometime earlier in the evening. They then looked at each other and commented on the enigma of what had just happened.

A few seconds later, things got much stranger for them as they both realized that their surroundings had become unfamiliar. Somehow, impossible as it appeared to them to be, they were no longer on Lake Pleasant Road.

John recalls looking at the dashboard clock at this point and noting the time as 1:14 AM. The clock supported their impressions that, even with the caveats of the sudden different environment and their seemingly abrupt stop in conversation, no time had passed for which could not be accounted. Also, the radio was not on for them to notice a skip in a song that might have otherwise been playing or any other similar indicator. In addition, there was no noticeable depletion in gas or any adverse effects on their vehicle, a 2003 Ford Explorer Sport-Trac.

And, although this may just be an interesting coincidence, adding to their feeling of disorientation, they noticed at their new location that there was a surprisingly high concentration of deer, accompanied by small animals, including a skunk and raccoon directly alongside, as well as crossing, the road.

Although John and his daughter were completely unaware of where they were after the momentary appearance of the fog, John felt it safest to continue on the route on which they found themselves. All they knew was that, according to the vehicle's compass, they were driving west at this time when they had been driving south. Within minutes, they discovered that they were somehow on nearby E. Newark Rd, on a stretch of road they rarely traveled.

As they drove forward, they arrived shortly at Highway M-24, a road they readily recognized. As they got onto M-24 and saw a sign indicating the city of Metamora was just south of them, they realized that they had mysteriously teleported several miles northwest of their original location. As John was a professional test-driver for Ford Motor Company at the time, he was particularly bewildered by this.

When they arrived home, both began to feel the onset of an unexplained mild tingling sensation throughout their entire bodies with a touch of nausea. This lasted until they fell asleep and was not present when they awoke. They were so shaken that Rose did not get to sleep until 4am, and John not until 9am. No other seemingly-related adverse or unusual sensations were felt by them at the time of the event or after.

There is no solid speculation of what happened to them, including any evidence of extraterrestrial involvement. Thankfully, it’s just a seemingly harmless mystery.

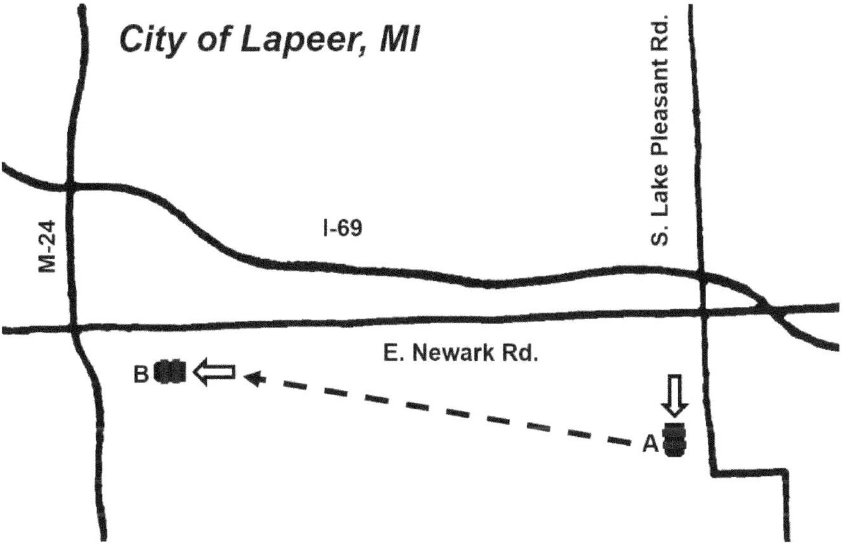
City of Lapeer, MI
S. Lake Pleasant Rd.
M-24
I-69
E. Newark Rd.
B
A

Experiencer 2

Part Two

Two Worlds Collide

Experiencer 2

Chapter One

After the Cloud

Experiencer 2

ONE. AFTER THE CLOUD

Summer, 1990 (Age 19)

It was just past 4am. I was outside in front of my suburban house with my small dog Sammy and there was a cloud above my house that wasn't a cloud.

The spectral thing in the air was flawlessly disc-shaped but wispy, subtly brighter than it should be against the night sky, and just hanging there. The wind was blowing and it wasn't affected at several hundred feet up, the only thing up there besides the summer stars.

Everything was silent as I stood roadside, unable to take my eyes off this curiosity floating unnaturally still, and I got the feeling it was somehow regarding me. My dog didn't seem to be nervous and I was under the assumption that dogs are supposed to be highly sensitive to strange vibes.

I suppose that if the oppressive atmosphere of dread that was pervading the kitchen ten minutes earlier while those beings were in the backyard regarding me didn't trigger Sammy (see *Raised in Two Worlds*), I guessed a peculiar-looking cloud probably wouldn't either.

My parents were still asleep upstairs in our tri-level home, completely unaware of the events of the last hour, as well.

The cloud was larger than the house. If it were to drop directly straight down, it would certainly have filled the property. But it seemed solid. Not a cloud somehow. Camouflage?

As I stared at it intently, waiting for a patch of mist to perhaps part somewhere on its surface and reveal something dark beneath, I detected the whole thing now slowly starting to move. Oddly, it was drifting into the wind, not with it.

The cloud picked up speed and moved with purpose upward and away from the house. It rapidly shrank away for several seconds in the night sky, then suddenly zipped off and disappeared at jaw-dropping speed. All that was left were the stars and I actually wondered if one of these was, in fact, the cloud's destination.

I didn't feel small and alone beneath the broad canopy of stars at that moment. I felt limitless. There was a connection between what I'd just experienced and the whole of the sky.

After a couple of minutes looking for any signs of movement in the heavens, I slowly started to walk back to my front porch, the surreal feeling dissipating. Although I knew the visitors were almost certainly gone from the back of the house, I didn't want to tempt fate and check.

Sammy and I stepped inside the darkened house and I trudged up the stairs to my bedroom, my legs starting to feel the first signs of tiredness.

As I entered my room, I set-up my usual locking mechanism, wedging a stick from my snare drum behind the adjacent dresser and in front of the door. I then walked to the window, closed it, and pulled the shades. Turning around, I switched on the floor fan that was pointed at my bed. If anyone stepped between the fan and me, the flow of air would be blocked, hopefully waking me.

I kicked off my shoes and crawled into my bed with my back against the wall, listening for any sounds, inside or outside. Eventually, the darkness slowly lifted with the onset of early morning and I heard my father's alarm clock. As I listened to him preparing for work, I felt safe and drifted to sleep.

A knock at my bedroom door roused me at a quarter after noon. Looking around the room, a wave of relief hit me as I saw the room bathed in sunlight. I was safe.

I opened the door a few inches until it hit the snare drum stick. I could see my Mom's face in the crack of the door, telling me that my friend Kyle was on the front porch to see me.

I got out of bed, carefully stepped around the intentional obstacle course of cluttered books and paper on the floor of my room, and walked downstairs to the front door. As it was summer and I slept in a t-shirt and shorts that passed for what I wore on any given day, I didn't have to take any effort to make myself presentable.

Through the screen door, I saw Kyle's tall and lanky form outside on the front porch. When he spotted me approach, he smiled and nodded. I stepped outside into the bright sunlight and looked past him to the street corner where I'd been standing mere hours before. It all seemed so different during the day.

I then told Kyle about the events of the previous night, not only about the strange cloud that flew at high speed against the wind but, more ominously, about the beings that were in my back yard just prior to that.

He listened intently but didn't say much.

Kyle had actually received his share of UFO strangeness himself. In fact, one strange event that he and I shared was in February of the previous year, our senior year of high school. He and I, along with our friend Don, had seen a strange display of lights in the night sky. First, a large, glowing blue ball arced over the car we were in, followed by a white light that zig-zagged about the sky, then a red ball of light briefly appeared and disappeared in the middle of the sky.

Back to the present, after he patiently let me relate the last night's events to him, he lightened the mood by alerting me to the upcoming 19th birthday party of our good friend TJ.

Instantly, I knew what he was announcing was significant in some way. In an odd way, perhaps this was something even somehow connected to the previous evening.

Often, there is a residual psychic effect to my high-strangeness encounters. It's a plugged-in feeling, alert to synchronicities with a slight boost to intuition. It diminishes slowly back to my normal degree of awareness over the course of a matter of days.

When Kyle told me of the party, it took little time to hone in on the psychic signal I was receiving and, in my mind's eye, I was clearly seeing Vicky, a casual friend of ours since our high school days. I asked Kyle if he thought she would be there and he replied by asking if this meant that I intended to ask her out on a date.

"She's going to be my girlfriend," I told him, matter-of-factly. While I'd actually never really thought of her like this before, I had no doubt or reservations that this was going to happen and that TJ's party would be the catalyst. It was fate. There was nothing I could do to change it.

And then another thought trailed behind it, a powerful intuition of upheaval in my life. Things were about to get unusual and things were about to get unpleasant. I could feel a static charge in the air as if two worlds were about to collide.

Chapter Two
The Gray House

Experiencer 2

TWO. THE GRAY HOUSE

Winter, Early 1991 (Age 19)

Snow crunched beneath my feet as I walked alone down the country road. The sky was much darker than I'm used to seeing in the suburbs and, what stars I could see through the dense trees, were brighter and more abundant. Bitter cold winds persistently whipped down the narrow lane and numbed my face. I wasn't really dressed well for the weather and a deep chill was taking hold of me.

As I realized that I needed to quickly find some shelter from the cold, it began to hit me that I wasn't sure where that would be. In fact, I must have been walking for some time but not sure where I was or why I was there. Nothing looked familiar and I unsettlingly couldn't remember back to even a few minutes prior.

I began to get nervous at the bizarre situation in which I found myself but thought that my memory had to snap back any second. This was just far too strange.

Up ahead, on the right, I spotted the tail end of a pick-up truck sticking out of the trees and realized that I was likely coming up on a home or cabin. On my approach, a small gray house became visible on the far side of the truck that was parked alongside a detached garage. The house lights were all off and I certainly didn't recognize the place. I considered perhaps knocking on the door and seeing if anyone was home so that I could warm up and get my bearings; however, the house didn't have a comforting vibe. Both the house and truck were covered in snow as if no one had gotten in or out of either in some time and, to top it off, I really had no idea what time it was.

As I trudged past the truck, peering at the windows of the gray house for even a glimmer of an active fireplace or a night light, I suddenly felt a sharp stare coming from the driveway and I stopped dead in my tracks. Turning my head quickly in that direction, I was confronted by a small charred gray being standing there, glaring at me.

I froze in place as its eyes flared up bright white and seared into my soul. Then, I shrieked explosively, not just with my mouth, but somehow with every atom of my being. My atoms roiled and I detonated with a furious cocktail of negative emotions…fear, sorrow, anger, horror, confusion, disgust, pain…even shame, jealousy, and guilt. I wailed these awful emotions out of me with a violent force until there was nothing left of me. I no longer existed.

Then, instantly, I somehow found myself in my bed at home, in broad daylight, out of breath and drenched with sweat. I looked over at the clock that said 2pm and heard a light knock at my bedroom door.

I stared at the clock silently in shellshock.

My bedroom door opened and my mother quietly walked in and dropped a letter on my chest and walked out of the room, shutting the door behind her.

The eyes of the gray being from in front of the gray house were still burning in my mind. "The creature," I kept repeating in my mind, "the creature."

"What just happened?" I wondered as I struggled for some continuity of events.

"I'm in bed and it's daytime…but it was just night and I was walking," I thought to myself.

"That wasn't just a dream. It was utterly real. The creature…the creature…disintegrated me. Am I dead?"

After several minutes of stupor, I rewound my day. It was a Monday and I recalled coming home from my class at nearby Macomb Community College and falling down for a nap only fifteen minutes before I awoke from what was not a dream.

I shuddered there several more minutes in confusion, not knowing what to do next. The words swirled in my head, "the creature...the creature" and then "disintegration."

It was then that I finally noticed the letter sitting on my chest. It was from my girlfriend of six months, Vicky. I opened it and the message said, "Dearest Bill, We had an amazing time together, but I need to be alone now. I'm sorry. You can call me if you want. Love, Vicky."

"Call the girl," my mind declared automatically. It was something to do. An imperative.

I got straight out of bed with a head rush and stumbled to the rotary phone on the desk in my parents' bedroom. My fingers fumbled as I dialed Vicky's number, all the while, my mind slowly repeating the mantra, "the creature...the creature."

"Hello," she said softly, almost in a whisper.

"Yes," I said. (in my mind... "the creature")

"Is this Bill?"

"Yes." ("the creature")

"Did you read my letter?"

"Yes." ("the creature")

"I'm so sorry. I sent that on Friday, but we had such a good time over the weekend that I realized I made a mistake. I don't want to break up anymore." Then, after a long pause, she asked, "Can you come over?"

"Yes." ("the creature")

"See you at 7?"

"Yes." ("the creature")

"Okay, I'll see you then."

"Yes." ("the creature")

"Bye."

"Yes." ("the creature")

Click.

What I should have been thinking is how awkward that Vicky knew that letter was on its way to me while we were in each other's arms the previous day. Instead, I fixated on the little gray being who ambushed me from the driveway of the gray house. The creature.

The confused terror that, at first, smothered me slowly alleviated over the next few hours and, by the time I was on the road to meet Vicky at her dorm room at Oakland University, my mind had refocused to my relationship with her in the context of the odd episode with the letter she sent me.

She and I had indeed hooked-up at my friend TJ's birthday party, just as I had predicted to Kyle the previous summer. The connection was effortless and natural. It was a good, light, summer romance, followed by an autumn where things settled into being serious and potentially long-term. She had, in fact, during this time, told me how certain she was that we'd marry.

Things sailed smoothly through the rest of the year and then found themselves at this uneasy point in early January, as I found myself driving to see her on a very strange day.

When I saw her, I didn't know what to say and we didn't really say much that night. I didn't tell her about my encounter with the creature from that afternoon, as she and I held one another in my car parked in the college parking lot. In one sense, we were already moving past the matter of the letter she'd sent; however, something was now shaken and unresolved in our relationship.

As I stared out the window into the night sky with Vicky beside me, my mind wandered back to the country road where the flash of the creature's eyes illuminated the darkness like the first bolt of lightning from an approaching storm. I believed there indeed was a deep meaning to the dreadful encounter I'd had that afternoon and that it would, before long,reveal itself.

Experiencer 2

Chapter Three
Autumn Apocalypse

Experiencer 2

THREE. AUTUMN APOCALYPSE

Fall, 1991 (Age 20)

Things began to take unexpected directions…and fall apart.

In the strange department, my friend Kyle, who had not previously had direct contact encounters to his knowledge, began having them after he, our friend Don, and I had our UFO sighting in February of 1989.

For starters (as I recount here from *Raised in Two Worlds*), in July of 1989, the three of us headed up to a secluded, densely wooded area outside of Traverse City, Michigan, to stay at a family home of one of our buddies. After an enjoyable day visiting the nearby Sleeping Bear Dunes, we retired back to the house. I slept on the floor in a pitch-black windowless room between Kyle, closest to the door, and our other friend closestto the wall. Don was also on this trip, sleeping on a couch in a separate room.

The following morning, Kyle reported something peculiar. He said that, in the middle of the night, someone came into the room and woke him up, asking, "Bill?" Due to the darkness, Kyle couldn't see who it was and couldn't identify the male voice. When Kyle groggily replied that he wasn't me, the unidentified voice said, "I'll be right back," and the individual hurriedly left with Kyle having no recollection of anyone returning. Kyle is certain it wasn't Don and none of the rest of us recalled anything unusual from the previous night.

Then things got even more direct for him.

One evening, after the sun had gone down, Kyle awoke from a nap at his girlfriend's house to see a rectangular portal of sorts hanging in the air right beside him, alongside the bed. Through this portal, he was able to see a wall covered in all sorts of electronics. Then, a small, bony hand reached out at him from one corner of the rectangle. He was unable to see more of the being. Trying to move away, he discovered he was paralyzed. Then a bright light bathed the room through the outside window as something was evidently rising up outside the house and into the sky. He could then move and the portal beside the bed was gone.

Another night, a couple of years later, Kyle was staying the night on a different girlfriend's couch in the basement while she slept in her room (she still lived with her parents), when he awoke to see two slim-figured individuals barely visible in the darkness watching him at close distance. The vague details he was able to ascertain were that the pair appeared to be Asian and that one was a taller female and, the other, a shorter male. He then quickly fell back asleep.

He also once had a vivid dream of the two of us in a car soaring above my home that he felt was potentially a real event.

Now, it was November 1991, and he had something he wanted to tell me.

It was ten months after my 'gray house' event and much had happened during this twentieth year of my life, not all of it good.

Vicky and I mutually decided to break up in August. It was uncomplicated and amicable. A key issue was that, although she was in college, her parents frowned on her dating. While she was away during fall and winter, living on campus, our relationship was easy to maintain. While she was home during the summer, every last second of contact between us had to be managed and usually hidden. If her parents (who were paying her tuition and on-campus room and board) suspected her of dating, they would have insisted she live at home during her college years. While I virtually lived with her on campus for the first few months of 1991, when classes ended in the spring, Vicky and I barely had any contact with each other.

My assumption at that time was that, after she settled back in on campus, we might perhaps pick back up at some point and keep going.

However, in November, I discovered that two guys from our close group of mutual friends who hung out with Kyle and myself several times a week had exceptionally intimate relations with her earlier in the year while she and I were still very much dating, starting pretty much immediately after she'd sent me the letter and then walked it back.

To make things worse, apparently, absolutely none of this was a secret to almost all of our extended group of friends. So, whenever I was out with this goup during the time that I was dating Vicky, most knew she was cheating on me with two friends who were often present…and, yes, she was often there with me.

When I finally made my rounds, asking why folks didn't tell me, they mostly all frustratingly said the same thing, "I didn't want to be the one to upset you.

With regards to the two friends who had relations with her while she and I were dating, it permanently dissolved one of these friendships and it took several years to mend the other. The friendship with the one that ended admittedly had much to do with the fact that he was actually quite happy to be a stinker. In fact, he went so far as to write a song about me which went something like, "You've got your head in a cloud. I have your girlfriend. Now, I'm the one who's proud." I had no idea he held such animosity (or wrote such bad lyrics). Off the list.

Instead of dwelling on the past, I decided to focus on developing the relationship with a girl I had casually started seeing after my break-up with Vicky…until that girl informed me she'd gotten back with an ex-boyfriend just two days after I found out about the Vicky shenanigans.

The next week my parents told me they were divorcing and selling the house where we lived and I had grown-up.

The entirety of my emotional support system became unstable over the course of two weeks: family, home, friends, love life. The Four Horsemen came to visit, if you will.

And on the topic of apocalypse, my connection to the Catholic Church was next. The Church taught me my whole life about good and evil, Heaven and Hell, reward and punishment. It would have been convenient to judge some of what had happened to me through this lens and feel righteously indignant. It would have been comforting to pray to Jesus for support. A giant monkey wrench got into the works, instead.

The final blow in my period of personal downfall came from a college professor who introduced our class that semester to the works of B.F. Skinner and his theory of Determinism, along with other thinkers with similar perspectives. An oversimplification of the basic shared theory states that the world is purely cause and effect. Everything happens because of the neutral chain of events preceding it. There is no freedom of choice. There is no good nor evil. Everything anyone does boils down to an automatic response to how he or she has been conditioned to operate by a combination of their environment and genetic predisposition. Everything is predetermined. Everything. This powerful and logical point of view blew my mind and caused a seismic and rapid paradigm shift within me.

Following this train of thought, everything bad that had just happened to me must have been destined to happen. Nothing anyone did could be singled out for blame because their actions were them simply acting out their conditioning.

This paralyzed me from doing anything about my situation. All I could do was sit in my room and connect the dots. This happened because of that, so, technically, I can't be upset. This person did that because of this other thing, so how can I be upset? I'm not saying that I identified myself as the cause in all of these timelines, just that I could see in some cases how a few of the key individuals were previously wronged in their lives at some point and looking for release.

Naturally, Vicky would want to get with any man she could if her parents completely prevented her from dating, even though she was an adult. Of course, one friend of mine with a rather strained family life probably would not know how to respect others' feelings. Certainly, my other friends would steer clear of involving themselves in the whole Vicky scandal for their laundry list of reasons. Etc.

There was rapidly so much stress from so many sources bottled up within me with seemingly no sensible emotional outlet. Did I have any ally in this that wasn't part of some of what was going on?

A correlation then came to my mind came of the gray house and the little gray man where I'd felt every negative emotion possible at once and, upon emotional release, felt as though I had died.

I wondered if it was possible that what I went through in my January experience was a portent from the beings, alerting me to my "autumn apocalypse." Was that really such a stretch? The message, if that's what it was, did place me alone in a strange, dark, and frigid place.

However much that did or didn't make sense, I needed something, so I went with that and put myself in their hands, mentally asking them to support me. I symbolically released my pain to them as I had done so actively and dramatically in January and rebooted myself on a foundation of faith that they had my back.

That backing came. In the aftermath of this melancholy time of my life, across several stunning events, it became all too apparent that they were with me and keenly interested in the direction my life was taking.

Experiencer 2

Chapter Four
Curious Laser Light

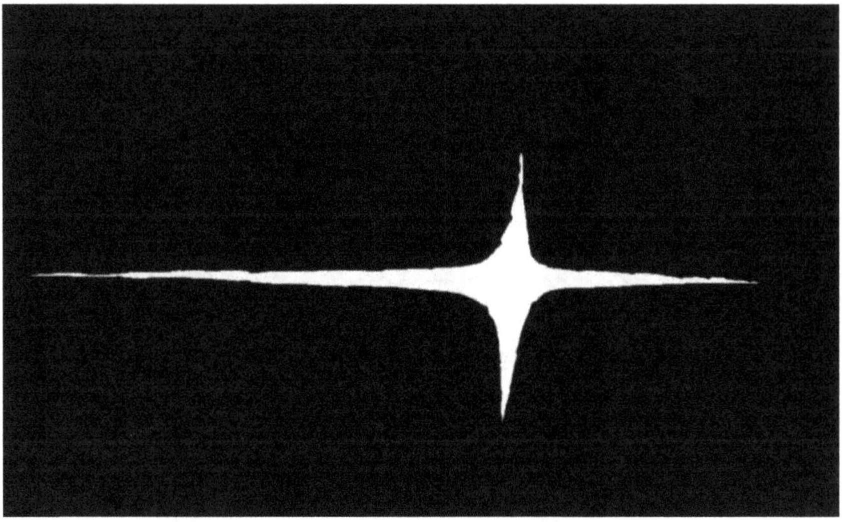

Experiencer 2

FOUR. CURIOUS LASER LIGHT

Summer, 1992 (Age 21)

I needed new friends. Certainly, the most grounded solution for me was to start hanging out with people who had nothing to do with the problematic group with whom I'd been running. Luckily, I did indeed meet some great and lasting friends during this time of re-adjustment. My old friendships were never abandoned but taking a break did wonders.

Some issues still lingered, though. I was emotionally still somewhat bruised and nowhere near ready to date again. One thing at a time.

Also, a change of company wasn't to say that odd phenomenon went away when I started to hang out with other folks. Thankfully, though, some of the things I experienced were relatively innocuous.

One quirky episode happened at a house that several friends of mine were renting in Ann Arbor while they were students at the University of Michigan.

I would occasionally visit them on weekends and, more often than not, crash on a couch. This particular night, I was in luck because one of the friends had gone home for the weekend and I was able to sleep in his room.

It was a warm night and I had the window open with just the screen. The curtains were open. As the window was at least ten feet above street level and the view outside was the windowless wall of the adjacent apartment building, I didn't need to worry about the late-night foot traffic of a busy college town looking in on me. The window was also at least a foot over me in the bed as I stared blankly into the dim room while trying to fall asleep.

Curiously, a tiny bright red dot appeared on the interior window-sill wall, as if someone was shooting a pocket laser up into the room from the street. I wondered what kind of goofball would think this was entertaining, but that thought only lasted a second, as the dot of red light began circumnavigating around *every* wall of the room in a clean, straight line at a slow pace. There was no shakiness of the light from an unsteady hand. The process appeared to be mechanical in nature. After the light reached the opposite edge of the window after making its way around the entire room, it exited.

I shot up and looked out the window, not seeing any evidence of its source.

This was impossible. The light traveled around the *whole* room. Even if someone did shoot a light up from the ground, how did they manage to hit the sections of the wall not visible from outside.

The next morning, I shared the event with my friends who didn't know what to make of it and added they knew of nothing else strange that had ever happened in the house. I also eventually asked the friend who stayed in the room if he was aware of anything in the house or whether anything unusual like this had ever happened to him in any capacity. He said no.

What in the world was this and what did it mean? Was something scanning the room? Was it meant as a message? A cosmic practical joke of sorts? I have no idea, but it did get my attention.

This was the straw that broke the proverbial camel's back and I thought to myself that there has to be someone reasonably local who investigates strange phenomena.

It turns out that one of my Ann Arbor friends who went home for the summer is from Chicago and I had a visit to her planned. Also in Chicago is the headquarters of the Center for UFO Studies about which I'd read. This is the scientific organization started by the late J. Allen Hynek to investigate the UFO phenomenon (and Hynek coincidentally investigated the dramatic 1966 UFO sightings in Ann Arbor). This would certainly be the place to start.

When the day arrived, I was nervous as I stepped into the modest CUFOS office and approached Dr. Mark Rodeghier, sitting a table surrounded by bookshelves teeming with books on UFOs.

I began by telling him about my 1989 UFO sighting with my buddies Kyle and Don.

Rodeghier replied by asking me if I'd reported this to my state MUFON chapter. MUFON? I'd never heard of it. He wrote down the phone number of Shirley Coyne and told me she was the Michigan State Director for the Mutual UFO Network.

When I got back home, I called Shirley and told her about the 1989 sighting and that I'd been having seemingly unexplainable things happen to me my whole life. She wanted to hear more and I gave her an earful. She then asked me to call her back on another day and go into more detail. On my third lengthy phone call to her, she asked if I would be open to hypnotic regression.

We met at her home for another discussion and several days later I was seated, under hypnosis, in a recliner at her home and recounting my earliest memory of contact with a gray being when I was only two years old (please see my first book).

In my following hypnotic regressions over the next year, there would be plenty more to tell Shirley, especially as my contact experiences were ramping up.

Experiencer 2

Chapter Five

Angel

Experiencer 2

FIVE. ANGEL

Summer, 1992 (Age 21)

I awoke in my bed to the feeling I was being watched. It was sometime in the middle of the night and my bedroom TV was somehow switched off (my mother possibly?). The room was being lit by the outside street light through the curtains.

In the dim light, I was puzzled to see a girl standing at my bedside. Then, as my eyes adjusted, I could make out three grays standing a few feet behind her, all silently staring at me.

For some reason, despite what would seem to have made for an alarming scene, I was not afraid. They all appeared to be in no hurry as if waiting for me to initiate something, whatever that might be.

I sat up and, during the silence, observed the girl closely. She appeared to be a teenager. Her skin was very pale and she had light-colored straw-like straight hair. Her most prominent feature was her unnaturally large dark blue eyes, only slightly bigger than a normal person's and nowhere near as large as the grays' eyes. She had a timid expression and posture and she wore no clothes.

So, this was a hybrid, I said to myself.

While I didn't get the impression that I was supposed to have some sort of intimate relations with her, I knew that she must be in my room for some reason.

After a prolonged awkward silence, with the ball apparently in my court, I asked the grays telepathically, "What's her name?"

They replied in joint telepathy, "Yes, what's her name?"

Was I supposed to name her? I mentally reached for the most innocent and flattering thing that I could call her.

"Angel," I said.

"Yes, Angel!" the grays replied telepathically in apparent delighted satisfaction.

Immediately, the four of them shifted sideways to their right in unison without moving a muscle, phasing out through the wall to the direction of the front yard. I didn't look out the window to see what happened to them after they went through the wall. My assumption was that I wouldn't see a thing.

For whatever reason, I was not at all shaken by their visit. I just dropped back in bed and felt a little sorry for this poor girl who seemed to have been hauled out to see me for the sake of the grays to witness both her and my reaction. My instinct was that she was probably raised in a controlled environment somewhere by the grays and was now being carted out to interact with humans for reasons known only to them.

This would not be my last experience with her, though.

Two years later, I awoke to find myself on board, standing in the room I've come to know as the "activity room." It's a large, empty, metallic-looking, round room with a high ceiling. An observation suite looks down on the room from one side.

As a handful of grays looked on, I was surprised to see Angel in the room, approaching me. She was still nude and looked about five years older than the last time I saw her, including having a more adult figure. I stood in place as she walked up and confidently made deep eye-contact with me. She then began to massage my temples.

I heard a telepathic comment from the observation suite, "This will get the blood flowing." Immediately, I began to lose consciousness as I felt my legs buckle and give out.

Many experiencers have had encounters with half-human/half-gray hybrid beings and I was aware of these entities before I'd met Angel. My story seems to differ slightly from what is normally reported in a couple of respects, though.

Angel is the only hybrid I recall ever meeting, and only in two encounters. A high percentage of experiencers who encounter hybrids report meeting several different hybrids over multiple encounters.

Reported encounters with hybrids can sometimes have a physically intimate nature. I have no feeling that anything more than what little I recall ever happened with me, nor do I feel I have any hybrid children or other hybrid relatives out there somewhere as other experiencers sometimes claim. My sessions with Shirley Coyne never revealed anything further, either.

Interestingly, though, in the spring of 2009, I hosted an experiencer gathering at my home. One of the attendees brought a sketchbook with her of encounters she'd had. I froze in shock at a picture she had drawn of the exact same activity room that I knew from being on board. She recalled there being no hybrids in her experiences in the room. As I recall, I believe she said they were testing her psychic abilities in some way. I had never told her prior to that of how I'd been in an identical room.

There are indeed times when another experiencer shares a recollection that you have also surprisingly encountered in your own life, be it a specific entity, location, or procedure. This is a double-edged sword. On the one hand, you breathe a sigh of relief from another person's identical (or near-identical) account. This external confirmation offers some evidence that a bizarre memory wasn't likely generated from your personal imagination. On the other hand, if you were holding out hope that you had possibly imagined whatever strange thing had happened to you, this external confirmation can make denial pretty challenging.

I'll never forget that afternoon of confirmation, nor the night the beings came to me with a nervous young hybrid.

While that particular late-night episode, being awoken from bed, wasn't particularly upsetting, when they woke me from my family room couch, two months later, it was an entirely different experience.

Experiencer 2

Chapter Six
The Book

Experiencer 2

SIX. THE BOOK

Summer, 1992 (Age 21)

One of the ways I would attempt to safeguard myself against abduction is to stay up late and outside of my bedroom. While not all events happened in my bedroom, the higher percentage of them did.

Watching late-night TV in the family room was one way to do this. As my older brothers had all already moved out of the house, I had it all to myself. Occasionally, I would drift off on the couch and awaken to the familiar sounds of my father getting ready for work in the early morning and I'd head to bed to finish whatever sleep I had left before I had to get up for a college class or for work.

This particular summer night of late-night television in June 1992 wasn't much solace against my fear of contact. After falling asleep on the couch, this time, I was surprisingly awoken by bright lights flashing intermittently onto my face.

I opened my eyes and groggily figured out that I was in the family room and that someone had turned off the TV. My parents would often just turn it off and leave me to sleep on the couch. It was clearly the middle of the night, but I had no idea of the actual time.

For some reason, multiple spotlights were rapidly sweeping the room through the bay window behind the couch I was on from a high position outside. This window looked out into the front yard. Curiously, even though there was a great deal of light, there was no sound. Everything was dead silent.

I lie still for what felt like roughly a minute, watching the light beams dance around the room until I mustered the courage to pop my head up and peek out the window. The lights were coming from several dark aircraft zipping by and doing incredible maneuvers at fantastic speeds, somehow managing to keep the lights focused on my house.

As there didn't seem to be any immediate danger, I decided to get a closer look at the aircraft. Very slowly, I crept to the front door and opened it. The light show continued unabated.

I became more curious than afraid. Also, for whatever reason, I chose not to wake my parents, asleep upstairs. I stepped outside, first briefly onto the front porch, then out into my front yard.

The craft were black isosceles triangles with small white lights at the rear vertices of the undercarriage and a single large maneuverable white light in the center that continued to point into my house. While the two front angles of these craft were straight lines, the rear side of them was a concave scoop. There were at least three of these craft, possibly more. As they had the capability of crossing from one horizon to the other in a matter of seconds, it was difficult to tell whether I was seeing the same ones returning or new ones flying overhead. The most that I saw at the same time was three. My impression is that they were the size of jetfighters but completely silent and persistently making impossible turns.

I stared up at them, dumbstruck, for several minutes, then felt an eerie chill of being watched from ground level.

Letting my eyes drop down from the sky, I saw a bullet-shaped metal dome parked on my front yard, about eight feet in height. There was a door on this dome and, standing in the door, was a tall gray. In his hand was a dull rectangular object that was the size of a large book. He peered intently at me and then began to slowly approach me.

I was suddenly terrified and turned toward my front door, but, as I tried to dash back into the house, I felt myself beginning to pass out. Soon, I was dragging myself up onto the porch. I made it to the door and looked back to see the gray still approaching.

"You must look at the book," he insisted telepathically. I understood that he was referring to the rectangular object he held and that it somehow contained some sort of information that I was supposed to see.

I stumbled through the door and closed it, immediately losing consciousness with the dreaded understanding that doors are not true barriers to these beings.

After passing out on the floor, I awoke the next morning in my bed, still dressed in what I wore the night before, with no further recall of what may have happened after I crawled into my house.

This event was re-examined soon after, during a hypnotic regression by Shirley Coyne. Unfortunately, nothing new came out of the session. My recall of that night still ended upon passing out after barely making into the house, even under regression.

Also, while I was about to enjoy a brief respite from the attentions of these entities, very Earthly beings were about to start behaving strangely around me.

Experiencer 2

Chapter Seven

Strange Calls

Experiencer 2

SEVEN. STRANGE CALLS

Summer, 1993 (Age 22)

I was at Lakeside Mall in Sterling Heights, shopping for neckties, and, after coming up empty-handed at my old workplace Crowley's, I decided to see what other stores had to offer. Much to my surprise, as I entered one of them where I never typically shopped, there was Vicky working. This is one of those coincidences that make you wonder if the universe enjoys playing practical jokes.

She and I hadn't spoken at all during the past two years since our break-up and my discovery of her antics. Unprepared to see her and not wanting to make a scene, I politely said "hi" and she replied by asking how I'd been doing. Although we hadn't seen each other at all during the recent years as I'd been successfully avoiding any potential encounter with her, we had a fair number of mutual friends and I'm sure she was aware that I knew much to everything that had been kept from me.

I said, "I'm better now," and, as if things were somehow normal and everything was casual, she started going into the minutiae of what she was up to lately. While looking for my exit from the conversation, her new boyfriend surprisingly showed up and provided an extended public display of affection as a clear demonstration to me that she was taken (because the universe apparently couldn't pass up an opportunity to crank up the gag). She gave no sign that this was awkward for her as she introduced me to him. I could tell he had no idea who I was from her past. "Good luck with that," I thought to myself for him as I made my polite escape.

Upon arriving home, I decided to call Kyle and share with him what had just happened. Then, while listening to his response, I was shocked to hear a recording of my own voice talking over his, repeating back to me a snippet of dialogue that I had said more than a minute earlier in the conversation. It only lasted about five seconds and Kyle didn't hear it. This was not an echo…unless the phone line can hold onto echoes for longer than a minute. Also, importantly, this was a pure landline to landline phone connection. 1993 was several years before everyone had cell phones or VOIP lines.

What did I say that was repeated more than a minute later? "She's not a bad person." To be clear, this recorded comment cut out right before I said the word "but" and followed up with a somewhat contrary assessment of her. Interesting edit, whoever did this.

While this is the only time I've ever discovered evidence of being secretly recorded on the phone, I found it weird that it had to do with Vicky, as if everything related to her wasn't already strange enough. Was I actually being bugged now that I was visiting a UFO investigator to hypnotically explore my encounters? I didn't think I was that subversive or fascinating and I doubt that anyone who would have been bored enough to track my life would've put any external connection together between my UFO experiences and Vicky, as I had done in my mind.

For what it's worth, to keep a gag running, Vicky's relationship with the boyfriend from the mall didn't last long and, years later, I am now friends with him as we share a number of mutual friends and, it turns out, he's a pretty cool guy. His wedding was a fun time.

Another situation involving the phone, though, a few weeks later, would be a little more unnerving.

My father had interviewed for a position at a potential new job while dissatisfied with his current employment. He gave the prospective employer our home number and they informed him to await a call from them on a particular date to let him know whether he was hired. As he would be at his current job when they were supposed to call, he asked me if I could be at home to take the call for him. As I had nothing lined-up for that day, that was fine with me.

It was early afternoon on the day of the expected call and I was sitting alone in the house reading Dr. David Jacobs' thought-provoking book on the alien abduction phenomenon, *Secret Life*.

The phone rang and it was my father asking if anyone had called for him. I told him no one had called and he asked if my mother, who herself was working that day, had perhaps taken the call. I clarified that no one had called at all that day and I was by myself. He then ended the call and I hung up.

Then, something felt wrong about me having said I was alone. I got a really bad feeling about saying that over the phone as if, even though it was the middle of a sunny, summer afternoon in a house along a busy road at the edge of a subdivision, that I had made myself suddenly vulnerable. I got goosebumps to go with a distinct feeling of being watched.

Shrugging it off, I walked back to the recliner, got comfortable, and picked the book back up.

Immediately, the phone rang again and I went and answered it. Dead silence. After several seconds of saying hello, I hung up, feeling a static electricity in the air, despite the July humidity.

Then, in the distance, I heard an approaching helicopter. This was not unusual, in and of itself. Helicopters passed over the neighborhood occasionally. In this case, though, the sound started to get surprisingly loud and close. It got to the point that the house's windows and knickknacks on the shelves were actually rattling and it felt like a helicopter was perhaps about to land on the roof.

I dashed outside, partly in fear for my life that I may be the victim of an aircraft accident.

Hovering directly over the house at excessively low altitude was a black unmarked Bell UH-1 "Huey" helicopter. As I stood out in my front lawn, being buffeted with a breeze from the helicopter's main rotor, the aircraft slowly climbed and headed east.

I watched it until it was a faint speck, then ran back in called Shirley Coyne as, coincidentally, she had told me that she had several encounters with very similar helicopters.

Her response was that I should call Selfridge Air National Guard Base, which was only about a dozen miles from my house, and complain that one of their aircraft flew too low to my home. I was understandably a little nervous about being so provocative to a military base, but she said it was the best way to show them I knew they were responsible and that I wasn't scared of them. She then told me to call her back after I spoke to them and she hung up.

While I really didn't know for sure that the base was responsible, the helicopter was indeed flying directly toward it.

I called and shakily made my complaint. The man on the other end said he'd look into it and call me back. Within minutes, he did, saying that there was indeed a helicopter at the time of my report headed toward Selfridge from Scott Air Force Base in Illinois, but that they're directed not to fly lower than 500 feet. I said it surely had and he replied that the pilot would be addressed. The call ended.

I called Shirley back and she seemed pleased that I had actually called them. For my part, I wasn't sure that I should've been so direct with them.

When my father got home that evening, I asked him if he had perhaps called the house back right after our first conversation and he said he hadn't. Unfortunately for him, the prospective new job called the next day to inform him that they had just hired a different candidate.

While I did my best to dismiss the human antics of the summer of 1993, the grays were about to reenter my life and step up their game.

Chapter Eight

White Space

Experiencer 2

EIGHT. WHITE SPACE

Fall, 1993 (Age 22)

I didn't know it at the time, but the afternoon hypnotic regression with Shirley Coyne would be my last.

As I drove to the Coynes' home that afternoon, I thought about which of my encounters we might discuss. We had covered so much in my previous regressions and there wasn't anything dimly lingering in the back of mind that I wanted to explore.

As I arrived, Shirley's husband George was lying on the couch in the front room, just outside the room where the hypnosis sessions were conducted, and he stayed there throughout our session.

What Shirley recommended when I got into the recliner was that I should simply ask my subconscious an open question to show me what I needed to see. She then induced me and I fell into a deeply relaxed state.

My mind swirled to pick out compelling signals as I sifted through snippets of memories onboard; however, each time I started to grasp onto a recollection, I felt a wash of disorientation blanket my thoughts that seemed somehow external and intentional. I tried and tried. I gave up trying and relaxed in surrender. That's when things got strange.

Curiously, the room started to get brighter through my closed eyes that I could no longer open. I started to feel physically lighter. Rapidly, the room grew so bright that it seemed like I was under a massive spotlight as my body suddenly felt as if I was floating upward. It seemed as though the walls of the room were actually beginning to fall away, leaving me floating in a white space apart from physicality.

Drifting in this space, I knew I wasn't alone. There was a presence of consciousness with me that had spirited me away to that place. It spoke telepathically to me.

"You always dwell on the negative. We are with you always and you are safe. We can see the entirety of your life and you will be fine. You persistently question whether we will return and there is no need to wonder…we will be back again and again."

Then, things started to dim and I began to feel heavy. The world was closing back around me and I felt thrown so violently back into the recliner that it hurt.

After what felt like about a minute, I was able to move and began to stretch my arms and legs.

Shirley remarked casually to me, "I lost you there for a little while."

I said, "I need to go to the bathroom," and dizzily staggered off to relieve myself.

As I stood in there, staring at myself in the bathroom mirror after washing my hands, through the thin wall of their home, I heard George say to Shirley, "There were three of them."

"What?" said Shirley.

"There were three of them standing at the end of the hall the whole time you were in there," George said, "They showed up a few minutes after you two went in and left a few minutes before you got out." Then it was silent. As if this all wasn't bizarre enough.

I exited the bathroom to join them and hear more.

As I entered the room with them, they were both staring blankly at me. Breaking the awkward silence, I said, "What's up?"

"Oh nothing," Shirley replied.

I said, "Oh, I thought I heard you talking about something."

"No. No," Shirley said politely and dismissively, followed by a long silence.

I realized they were not going to tell me.

The oddness factor was too much for me and I said, "I have to go," and headed straight out the door for home, thanking her on my way out.

As I lie down that night with the bedstand light and bedroom television on, my usual comforts to help allay my fear of falling asleep and possibly being abducted, something surprising happened. I felt as though I didn't need these security blankets. Somehow, for reasons still unknown to me, the message from my hypnosis session and whatever that was that happened to me during, relaxed me, even though the last words were that they would indeed return.

I switched off the television and light and slept soundly.

Furthermore, ever since, I have had no problem going to bed without lights, television, radio, fan, windows closed and curtained, obstacle course on the floor, dog in the room, and barricade on the door. Those years were behind me.

This would be the last time I would ever see George and it would be years before I saw Shirley again, as she left MUFON and found a new husband after George passed a few months later. I never did hear more from her about the beings in her home that day and she has now passed, too.

The beings weren't done delivering very personal messages, though, and the next ones would occur back in my bedroom.

Experiencer 2

Chapter Nine

More Messages & Moldavite

Experiencer 2

NINE. MORE MESSAGES & MOLDAVITE

Winter, Early 1994 (Age22)

It was just over two years since my "autumn apocalypse," and I was still living in the same impossible-to-sell house with my parents who were now divorced and sleeping in separate rooms of the same tri-level home. It goes without saying that this was a somewhat awkward existence, waiting for the house to be sold so that my parents would know how much money they'd have to split to find new living arrangements apart from each other.

After dinner, one evening, I relaxed in bed to take in some light reading. I was lying with my head at the foot of the bed to catch the last of the sunlight that came in through the window. After several minutes, I became drowsy and fell asleep.

I awoke to the surprising sound of a man's voice speaking. My eyes wouldn't open for some reason. The sun had apparently gone down while I'd slept and now the room was dark beyond my closed eyelids. To my dread, I discovered I couldn't move at all.

The voice sounded professional, like a newscaster, and I thought for half a second that it was my bedside clock radio; however, the voice was coming from directly above and behind me while my radio was at the other end of my bed.

In addition to the voice, I also recognized the sounds of the TV playing downstairs. These were both clear audio signals at different volumes from different directions.

An even stranger detail about the voice was that when I tried to concentrate on what he was saying, his voice became quiet and indistinct, preventing me from understanding what was being said; however, when I loosened my focus, the voice became louder and clearer until I again tried to catch any of the message in vain. Frustratingly, I couldn't catch a single word.

After what felt like about three minutes of this, the voice began to fade, but before it disappeared completely, I heard one clear message, "Wherever you go, we'll be there," and I was slowly able to move and open my eyes. I lie there for a few more minutes, listening to the television downstairs before I got up and left my bedroom.

Later that week, our house found a buyer.

Moving out of the only house in which you've ever lived is quite a change when you'd spent your first twenty-plus years there. Luckily, ever since my encounter in the white space while I was at the Coyne's home, my bedroom was relatively uncluttered as I no longer felt the need to make the room I slept into an obstacle course to try to deter the grays.

It was just two days before the move that my missing moldavite from six years prior shockingly reappeared on my bedroom dresser. Please see my first book for the full details on that, but the short version is that I'd bought three pieces of moldavite while I was in high school that all disappeared under curious circumstances within the house. As mysteriously as it had disappeared, the last piece returned after six years, just in time to accompany me to my new home, a condo I would share with my Mom for a couple of years before I graduated college and moved out into an apartment.

I've always had a special relationship with moldavite. This green glass gemstone fell to earth in an asteroid roughly 15 million years ago, making it literally extraterrestrial.

At the risk of waxing a bit cosmic, I'll confess it clearly has an amplifying effect on my energetic connection to the universe, more than any other crystal or stone that I've encountered. I feel plugged-in through moldavite when I hold it or wear it. It pushes warm vibrations through me and I feel somehow visible to higher forms of consciousness. In fact, the power of it is so strong that I still only wear it when I'm in a very grounded, positive, and meditative mood out of concern of what might happen if I were to be connected to it while excited or depressed.

After I wrote about moldavite in my first book, where I also included a similar story from a friend about its penchant to vanish, I've heard from several people who have their own moldavite stories. A few of these individuals had even experimented with acquiring some after reading my experiences and wanted to share with me what had happened to them.

There is indeed an eerily high number of accounts of people I know who lost their moldavite under questionable circumstances. One friend of mine even had two disappear at once out of a small bag full of other crystals that he carried around with him. I was shopping in a store one day where I complimented an employee on his moldavite hanging on a necklace, to which he replied that he had actually purchased one for his wife and one for himself, but his had oddly gone missing and he was wearing hers. He, of course, had no knowledge of my own curious stories. These are just two accounts of many.

I still have no idea why moldavite goes off on its own…and where it goes…and why and how one piece of moldavite would find its way back to me after several years right as I was moving out of the house where it previously disappeared.

Much like the reappearing moldavite, what was about to happen next was years in the making.

Experiencer 2

Chapter Ten

Night of the Phoenix

Experiencer 2

TEN. NIGHT OF THE PHOENIX

Winter, Early 1995 (Age 23)

The climax of five years of strange events was finally upon me. One weekend at the beginning of 1995 would bring simple but dynamic closure to the odyssey of life-changing personal and paranormal incidents I'd been living for the past several years.

TJ invited me to spend a weekend ski get-away at his cabin in Lewiston, in the area of Michigan's lower peninsula colloquially known as Up North. There would be an estimated group of about ten in attendance and the trip would be in late January.

I readily agreed. Then, he said his broad invitation list included Vicky, with whom he was still friends. He'd been friends with her since elementary school, so what could I say. While I had been up to his cabin several times, she never had, so I bet on the likelihood she'd decline his offer, especially after she found out I would be coming. It was one thing for her and I to chat for a minute in a shopping mall but quite another thing to be in the same small cabin in winter for a whole weekend.

Then, surprisingly, she ultimately did decide to come...along with her new husband Vince, whom I'd never met, an additional twist. So, she and I knew each other were intending on coming, but neither of us blinked.

Besides myself, the final list included TJ, his brother and sister, four friends not around for the original drama from three years earlier, and Vicky and Vince.

As I pulled up to John's house on Friday evening of the trip to figure out carpool between our three selected vehicles, I was met in the driveway by TJ's sister. She said she felt that I should have the opportunity to see Vicky's husband Vince from a distance before I formally met him. I thought this was an unusual approach until I looked through the front window of the house and saw him. He was aggressively disheveled in appearance, in fact, aggressive-looking in general. This was a shock to me how someone like her could have fallen for someone like him, assuming he must be quite the bad boy charmer. As it would turn out, he was far from charming. He was distant and confrontational with everyone. As I was luckily not in the same car as him, I didn't suffer the misfortune of his better acquaintance until we arrived at the cabin.

Friday night started off well enough, apart from Vince quickly shedding his shirt and keeping it off for much of the weekend. I'm not one to talk, but no one appreciated him going for that choice.

He was also loud and judgmental. His conversational style began with interrogation and ended with a sharp dismissive appraisal of anyone he could corner. He was certainly not there to make friends.

Saturday morning, he volunteered to go for a beer run and collected everyone's money, then got the most inexpensive beer he could find (in this case Carling Black Label). When he got back and we questioned his purchase, he boasted that, this way, he would be able to pocket the most amount of money from the deal. We were in our early twenties, so we drank the beer, anyway.

While I could go on, I will wrap-up the description of his antics of how, after eating a bowl of home-made chicken noodle soup that one of the group generously prepared, he decided to pour the remaining broth from his bowl back into the half-full pot of soup. I think this paints the appropriate picture.

Vicky, for her part, was also distant but thankfully quiet, rarely speaking to anyone but Vince. Her presence was awkward but never created a difficult situation. She spent the majority of her time away from everyone, parking herself either in the corner of the room or in bed.

As our group was somewhat large for the cabin, we had to be creative with sleeping arrangements. Vicky and Vince took the master bedroom, and while others took the bunk beds and fold-out couch, I put the deck recliner cushions that were inside for the winter into the bathtub and slept just fine. As the water was shut off for the winter, there would be no one wanting to use the facilities and I enjoyed my own private bedroom.

Saturday was ski day. Vicky and Vince blessedly stayed at the cabin while everyone else hit the slopes for the day. The outing had a surprising big finish for me as, on the last run, I accidentally twisted around shortly after I started off and I skied down the majority of the hill backward, complicated by the fact I couldn't see due to continuously kicking up a spray of snow off the back (front!) of my skis. Luckily, I hit no one and nothing and miraculously survived completely unscathed with a great story. This was a strange weekend, about to get much stranger.

The group returned to the cabin to kick back for some Black Label and relaxation until quite late.

As the last us finally called it a night and I settled into my tub bed, I began to hear playful flirting and giggling through the thin wall that separated the bathroom from the master bedroom. I was mortified that I had fallen so low as to suffer this. Then things got worse. Vicky and Vince proved to be exceptionally vocal lovers.

There I was…in a bathtub…in the middle of the night…hours from home…while the ex-girlfriend at the epicenter of my emotional breakdown was loudly amorously engaged in the next room with the most unfortunate choice of a husband.

If there was ever an example of "so bad it's funny," this was it. I couldn't control myself and started to snicker, then chuckle, then lost it, soon laughing uncontrollably as tears streamed down my face. The heavy weight that had held me down for years was growing lighter and lifting off my chest. I felt remarkably full of joy and absolutely ecstatic. As I couldn't stop laughing and was now completely energized (even despite my day of skiing), I leaped up, grabbed my boots, and ran out the front door of the cabin into the snowy night.

I kept running and laughing loudly down the snow-covered dirt road, past occasional neighboring cabins, until I was winded and had to switch to a walk. Then, when I realized I was rather far from the cabin, a strange feeling of déjà vu came over me. Why did walking alone down a rural road in the middle of a snowy night seem so oddly familiar? Then, it hit me.

To my right was a gray cabin that exactly matched the one from my experience from four years prior. And standing in the driveway was…

No one.

I felt as if I stood in two times, separated by years, but deeply connected. It was electrifying and more real than real. I felt as good at that moment as I'd felt bad during the experience four years prior. This place was ground zero of my heart's demise and rebirth. I was back and fully alive.

It appeared the beings knew four years earlier that a chain of events had been set in motion at that time that would resolve on this trip.

I walked back to the cabin a new man. Everyone was snoring peacefully when I walked back inside as I felt the warmth of the space heaters beginning to thaw my smiling face.

Slipping back into the bathtub, I slept perhaps the best that I had in years, and couldn't wait to get back home and experience life in this wonderful new state.

Unfortunately, the grays weren't done with getting involved with my relationships, just yet, or blowing my mind with surreal experiences.

Chapter Eleven

The Silent Hill

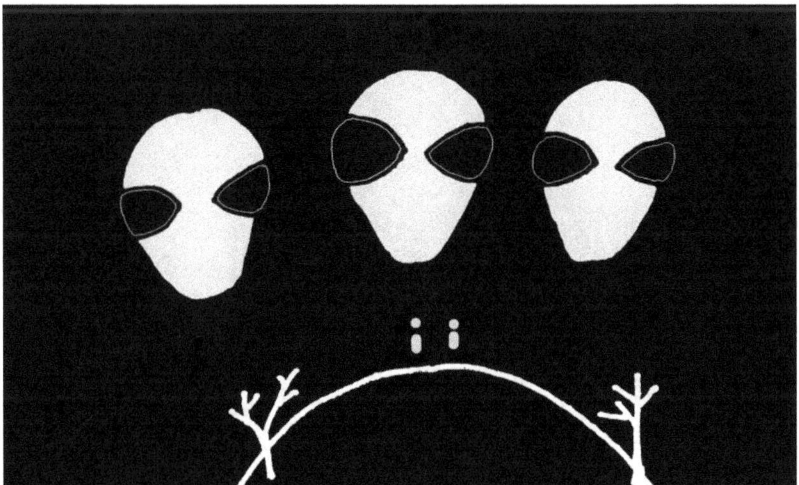

Experiencer 2

ELEVEN. THE SILENT HILL

Spring, 1995 (Age 24)

I was liberated. The crushing weight was off my chest and the fog was gone from my mind. Everything around me looked so different and bright. I could feel the capacity to love again thawing within me and I had no interest in hibernating any longer.

It wouldn't take long to re-enter the world of dating. I was at a party at a friend's house in March of 1995 when a friend of a friend named Tammy took an interest in me. She was energetic, graceful, and very sweet. We started going out and, as things steadily progressed over the following months, one issue was gnawing at me…

There comes the moment when you have to tell the person you're dating that you are an abductee. An important reason, of course, is if they don't believe you or have an issue with your situation, it can quickly sweep the legs out from beneath a budding relationship. An even more important reason is that, at some point, they may happen to be present for one of your encounters.

One issue with telling them too soon, though, is that you may scare them off before they get to understand you're not crazy. Timing is everything and, two months in, I was not yet quite ready. In this case, though, I apparently wouldn't have any control over that.

What happened is somewhat complicated to tell because it was a complicated matter. Also, to be clear, no alcohol or illicit substances were involved. We weren't into anything harder than beer and didn't drink at all that day, anyway.

We decided to go hiking at the Holly Recreation Area, in Holly, Michigan, a large park about an hour from Sterling Heights, where she and I both lived. The day was warm and sunny and we covered much of the park through the afternoon and early evening. We weren't yet ready to leave and identified a nice large hill off-the-beaten-path that afforded a good view of the setting sun. We spread out a blanket that we'd brought for our afternoon picnic and sat there until the stars came out.

When darkness came, as we lie embraced on the blanket, there was a stark and sudden hush in the ambient noise of the surrounding woods. The frogs and everything else went silent. This was followed by the unmistakable sound of approaching footsteps crunching branches and trudging through leaves, coming up the side of the hill where we were situated. Whoever or whatever it was would reach us in a matter of seconds.

We leaped up and hurried to the center of the hill, looking back and waiting to see what or who would break through the trees. Nothing came out and the sound of footsteps stopped. Then, the natural noises of the woods suddenly returned.

After waiting nervously for a couple of minutes, especially since we didn't hear footsteps going back down the hill, we tried to start up some small talk with one another.

Tammy started by pointing out what she thought was the Big Dipper. I corrected her that it was the Little Dipper and started to discuss the recent college astronomy class I'd taken. Conversation then segued to the high cost of college textbooks.

After that, we decided to return to the blanket and we reclined on it once more.

After a few minutes, though, the park again became eerily quiet, followed by the sound of approaching footsteps.

Once again, we got up and moved to the center of the hill. She called attention to what she thought was the Big Dipper. I corrected her, talked about my astronomy class, and then we lamented the price of college textbooks. Somehow, this gave me a sense of déjà vu, but I honestly had no recall at that moment that this was the second time we had done any of this. Tammy also gave no sign that she thought anything was perhaps amiss.

Then, the sounds of nature returned and we returned to the blanket...until the sounds stopped again and the footsteps approached once more.

We walked quickly to the center of the hill and discussed the Big Dipper, Little Dipper, my astronomy class and the price of textbooks.

Once again, the déjà vu hit and I was about to ask her if she had the same feeling...then, before I could ask, it hit my memory clearly that we'd had this conversation (at least) twice, already. Outlandishly, it seemed that we were in some sort of time loop!

It was too late. I found myself standing completely immobilized, staring face-to-face with Tammy, who was also completely frozen, as now several sets of footsteps approached up the hill.

Three small gray beings emerged from the shadows, walked directly toward Tammy, surrounded her, and began inspecting her up and down.

I was terrified and started to horribly regret not having left the park earlier. How stupid I was to have put us in this situation.

The grays then began to telepathically communicate with one another, saying things like, "No, not her," and "She's no good for him," and "She's not the one." If I could hear their telepathic chatter, I also wondered if Tammy could.

After a few brief minutes, the beings casually strolled back down the hill. About a minute after that, Tammy and I could move again...and move we did.

We grabbed our blanket and backpacks and ran the half-mile back to my car without stopping, hopping in and speeding away as fast as possible.

We were absolutely quiet in the car until we approached her home. Even though it was now approaching her curfew time of midnight, she requested that I not drop her off yet.

I thought it might be best if we go someplace where there were other people and I pulled into the parking lot of a Meijer store. It seemed to be just the place. Open twenty-four hours, big and brightly lit, and always with a fair number of people inside at any time of the day, made it a perfect choice.

We walked in and randomly shuffled slowly through the aisles, staring intently at and sometimes picking up and examining items like mops, magazines, toothbrush holders, etc. Essentially, we were grounding ourselves through common items of consumerism.

After a while, we found ourselves in the pet department where the hamsters were awake and active. We both sat on the floor and watched them for about twenty minutes before Tammy said, "Okay. I think I can go home now."

We left Meijer and I dropped her off at her place. She exited my car with a despondent distant gaze and trudged to her door without looking back.

We didn't speak for two days when she called and asked me to please come over to talk. Immediately, upon my arrival, she broke up with me. We didn't discuss the events in the park then and wouldn't ever again. While I never told her what we went through had anything to do with me, I suspect she knew it had everything to do with me.

I wouldn't be deterred from dating again, though. Happy endings are possible, even when your life is punctuated by dramatic and unusual events.

Chapter Twelve

Happily Ever After

Experiencer 2

TWELVE. HAPPILY EVER AFTER

Winter, Early 1996 (Age 24)

While reading a newspaper in the early afternoon of January 6, 1996, I received a call from Kyle. He asked if I would like to join him to play laser tag that evening with a college buddy of his. I readily agreed, especially as I hadn't seen or heard from Kyle since the summer of 1995, which was actually the longest span of time at that point that we'd ever been out of contact. We weren't avoiding one another, just living the busy lives of mid-twenty-somethings and had our own stuff going on.

After I hung up the phone, I returned to reading the paper and got to the horoscope section. I never really made it a point to seek out newspaper horoscopes, nor did I often even read a newspaper at that age.

My Aries horoscope for the day read, "You will reunite with an old friend. Avoid any new business prospects. You will meet a new love interest." I thought this was a rather ambitious list for one day. Then, I realized that I had already, in a way, reunited with an old friend. Kyle and I would have reconnected anyway at TJ's cabin a few weeks later for the annual winter gathering (Vicky was not invited), but this was an excellent opportunity to catch-up.

That night, we had a good time playing laser tag and headed over to the local Chili's restaurant for a late meal. Right after we were seated by the hostess, Kyle's buddy asked us if we would be interested in participating in a business project with him. He was selling long-distance phone service and we would work under him in a multi-level marketing model. Instantly, I thought of the second part of my horoscope and declined the business proposal.

So, that was two out of three with the "new love interest" prediction still pending. While I was very much open to the idea, especially since I hadn't dated steadily since my break-up with

Tammy the previous spring, it was already 10pm, and I would surely be heading home after leaving the restaurant.

Our server showed up and I was surprised to see it was Becky, one of the members of our extended group of friends. I asked her if she was going to TJ's cabin in a couple of weeks for the weekend trip and she replied she wasn't sure and hadn't yet asked for the time off. She took our food orders and headed back to the kitchen. A couple of minutes later, she returned to say that she'd just gotten the time off and would be going on the trip.

Two weeks later, Becky kissed me on the cheek at TJ's cabin. We began dating and ultimately got married in May, 2001. Currently, we live in a creatively laid out gray house (no, not that one).

My involvement with the Mutual UFO Network grew and I became State Director of the Michigan Chapter in 2004. At the time of this writing, I still hold this position. In this role, I have connected with hundreds of other experiencers and been blessed with the opportunity to hear the many accounts of others and share my own.

The events covered in this book don't mark the end of my curious experiences, but this does wrap-up the storyline of my early twenties, when beings from elsewhere took a deep and active interest in my humble personal life, before stepping back, apparently satisfied, and letting my life flow.

Part Three

Reflection

Experiencer 2

PART THREE. REFLECTION

Reviewing the events that happened during this six-year period of my life is understandably challenging for me. It is tough enough to revisit and sort out for my personal reflection, let alone share it with others. Furthermore, I am not a cutting-edge scientist, equipped to explain how several of the things I went through are possible because of this or that quantum or multi-dimensional what-not. At best, I can hopefully pose some reasonable questions. I will examine here a few of my strange episodes with a little more depth, but please don't anticipate answers. I'm just as baffled as anyone who has read up until this point.

THE GRAY HOUSE

As to the matter of the Gray House experience that I had in 1991, where I found myself in another location at a different time, what can be made of that?

What must have been a dream wasn't a dream. I've had vivid dreams (and really vivid dreams), but this was not like that. It was a full-sensory experience with continuity of clear-headed thought and time flow. The environment was persistent with no anomalies (apart from the gray being). I felt and heard the wind through the trees and the snow crunching underfoot. When I breathed, the air was cold. My train of thought was steady and consistent with my waking consciousness. I was absolutely there in the most real sense possible.

Also, of course, there is the matching reality that I relived four years later, exactly as I remembered it (apart from the gray being). While I'd been to my friend TJ's cabin a number of times since first having visited Lewiston in 1989, I don't recall having been on that nearby road where I found myself until winter 1995.

Was my 1991 consciousness going for a ride in my 1995 self, somehow? If so, why didn't a gray being appear in the 1995 version of events? Also, my 1995 self was intensely aware of the 1991 self seeing the gray being where the 1995 self did not, creating a trippy feeling of being in two times simultaneously.

With the 1991 event anchored to the beginning of an emotional rollercoaster that ended with the 1995 event, what does that mean?

Were the beings looking at my life in 1991 and actually caring enough to step in to try to support my fragile human ego? Deceit from one's friends during a period of instability in life is a pretty rough ride, but is it enough for entities from another planet to care in the least?

Maybe they wanted me alive for something and were looking to ensure my depression wouldn't permanently derail my life.

One wild-card thought is they wanted to make certain that I passed along a line of DNA that they'd been studying for generations. Perhaps, this isn't really far-fetched, considering how the phenomenon runs in my family and that they openly disapproved of compatibility with Tammy in 1995 (for what it's worth, I don't believe she ever had children of her own).

Another thought, strange and humbling to consider, is that they were grooming me to speak publicly about my experiences. They wanted me to share what happened to me to help keep them in human conversation. Other experiencers have expressed this same sentiment about themselves.

I don't take this to mean I see myself as somehow exceptional in any way. I just happen to have the opportunity to speak on something that most who have had this nature of experience cannot due to the difficulty that would follow with their family, friends, or work. It would be great if the general public were at a better place with this, but until we get there, those of us who can speak, ideally, should speak. I make no apologies for who I am, what I do, or how it appears, when I represent this phenomenon.

The other category of why they would get so directly involved with certain individuals is out of some sense of personal connection with or affection for us. I cannot deny that, in my circumstances, they appear to care. If another human had done so much for me, my gratitude would likely come naturally and not with such a clinical review of motivation.

THE BOOK

On the night that I awoke on the family room couch to the lights of triangular craft zipping through the sky and a domed pod parked in the front yard, there was a mystery I wonder if ever will be solved. What was this box that the being from the pod called a book?

I can fathom a guess that it contained some sort of informational content that I was supposed to absorb but not readily remember. This aspect of the contact phenomenon is not uncommon. Many experiencers claim they have memories of being taught things that are locked into a form of mental quarantine that they are unable to access until some fated promised day when the beings claim it will be important.

Many times, these experiencers have a vague recollection that their lessons are focused on some upcoming calamity that will affect human survival and that they are expected to apply suddenly accessible long-forgotten teachings to help at least some people make it through whatever disaster.

There is a curious side to this. So many experiencers making such claims to date have passed away without ever fully unlocking what they've been taught. How good of prognosticators are these beings if they are giving practical future information to carefully selected individuals who won't be around for this predicted future?

Experiencer 2

I suppose one thought on this is that the beings don't absolutely know if or when their view of the future will necessarily come to pass and only have a percentage of certainty. They then take out an insurance policy. This is done by secretly embedding instructions in the minds of multitudes of experiencers of what to do in the case of one or more catastrophes. These memories become unlocked to select living experiencers if a given situation unfolds. Otherwise, the instructions stay forgotten for life rather than confuse or upset the experiencers.

WHITE SPACE

What really happened during the hypnosis session that I had where I ended up floating, seemingly disembodied, in a white space while three entities waited in the home of my hosts?

The impression I received is that I had an out-of-body experience that was instigated and directed by a higher conscience. It appeared to have been orchestrated to make me a captive audience while I received a message as directly from the source as possible, cutting through all pretenses of physical form and making a connection of pure spirit.

I have proposed before that I suspect consciousness is the native form of these beings and that they only become physical in the instances that require it.

Their contact with me that afternoon was as dramatic a show as possible…during a hypnosis session intended to learn more about them… with a witness observing three physical entities in the next room!

Why were the physical beings there? Perhaps to somehow ensure that the session wouldn't be interrupted? Perhaps to be on-hand to restore me to my body should something in the process go amiss? Perhaps so that there would be an outside witness to the event in some manner so that I wouldn't merely shrug off the event as purely my imagination?

In any case, the encounter was remarkably effective in easing my tension about their promised visitations in the future. I've been able to sleep soundly without added securities or comforts, ever since.

THE SILENT HILL

The encounter on the hill in the park was bizarre for many reasons.

It was such a perfect set-up to isolate an experiencer and potential mate for a snap inspection. Were they so vigilant of my daily activities that they were able to execute an impromptu landing? Did they know we would be there that day? Did they somehow arrange it?

On that last thought, this would certainly take an incredible exercise of both logistics and telepathic prodding on their part.

If they arranged it, they would have needed to determine an environment where she and I would be alone and that they could discreetly land their craft. They absolutely demonstrated expert precision on this score. We were alone, in the woods, on an isolated hill, in the full darkness of night, with warm weather and a clear night, next to a large open field for their craft. You couldn't have done a better job here.

Secondly, they would've needed both of us to want to put ourselves in this scenario. I would've had to think their idea was my idea about where she and I should go, what day we should go there, and that we should, at the last minute, extend our stay there until nightfall. Then, she would have had to agree with all of this.

All of the above would be a heck of a lot of planning if this was orchestrated by them. Admittedly, it may have only required planting the seed in our heads to stay there later than we originally planned after they'd figured out what a perfect set-up into which we'd put ourselves. It's so easy to overthink this, but curiously undeniable how much everything was to their advantage.

While she and I were frozen in place and they were inspecting her, I wonder what criteria they were using to judge her. I highly doubt they gave any thought to her looks. They seemed to be psychically scanning her for something intangible.

Were they trying to determine if she was psychologically compatible with their ongoing presence, as in, would she be accepting of or antagonistic toward them if she and I were to become lifemates?

As mentioned previously, were they trying to determine if she was a good vehicle to produce a baby with DNA favorable to their program?

Were they looking for something that is beyond human comprehension?

The fact they said, "she's no good for him (me…not them)," is certainly interesting.

When the beings came up the hill, why did all the ambient noises of the surrounding woods go quiet? This strange phenomenon of corresponding stillness around contact experiences is actually commonly reported. There are disorienting effects sometimes referred to as the "Oz Factor" (named after author L. Frank Baum's fantastical land of Oz, as if the experiencer has suddenly found him or herself in a separate, magical reality). The Oz Factor can represent a wide array of mystical sensations and a sudden hush over the environment is one of them.

How might the beings cause all things to go silent in a projected area, or at least mess with the heads of experiencers to make them believe that the rest of the world has gone quiet? And what is the value of this if it is an intentional effect? Half-jokingly, perhaps flying saucers are exceptionally loud and it's a broad noise-dampening measure. Perhaps the silence is an indicator that the experiencer has briefly left the physical? If it is somehow an unintended effect, what kind of life form or technology would unintentionally broadcast a zone of silence?

Another highly speculative thought on this is that everything goes quiet because time itself is paused. It would obviously be a herculean effort to stop all of time and I have serious doubts that they could do this. On the idea that they stop time only in a fixed area, would the universe comply to being so acutely disrupted? A stranger point to this still is that time is not completely stopped if the beings can still move about freely. How is that possible?

But, wait, there's more. This leads to the biggest can of worms. The time loop.

How did time loop? Why did time loop?

Firstly, did time actually loop…or were Tammy and I just compelled to repeat our actions (strange enough on its own merits)? Perhaps they wanted to orchestrate our placement on the hill (standing apart, not laying near one another) but had trouble getting the timing of our positioning right in relation to when they showed up?

But what of the sound of the footsteps coming up the hill being part of the repeated sequence? Wasn't that them actually approaching? Unless that sound was a telepathic ruse to get us to move and there really wasn't any of them approaching at that moment (correction…moments!).

What if they just made us both think we were repeating our behaviors and we actually only went through the sequence once? Why would they do that, though?

One could go bonkers playing this guessing game.

If it was an actual time-loop, that would mean a mastery of time beyond just pausing it. This power would indeed be Godlike…and quite a bit of overkill to briefly snare a couple of harmless twenty-somethings.

I can think of no good reason for either time to have looped or for them to have tricked us into some sort of amnesiac game of repeating our behaviors, but these two explanations are unfortunately the leading candidates.

ANGEL

When I was awoken by grays who had brought along a hybrid, I asked them her name and they replied back to me, "What's her name?" I still believe they wanted me to name her, but their behavior also matches something puzzling I've seen about them in how they manage the present moment.

While the beings appear to swim freely in an ocean of consciousness, seemingly aware of every bit of time and space simultaneously, the small grays, in particular, occasionally display a strange behavior when walking in the physical. They sometimes appear to be hyper-focused in the moment when they're asked questions.

Whenever I am lucid enough to ask them things like, "Where are we going?" they telepathically respond, "We're going." "Why are you doing this?" gets a response of, "We're doing this." I don't think they're being coy. Honestly, I believe that's what's going through their heads, almost as if their entire mental process is locked in that precise second.

It's as if that, when condensed into physical form, they paradoxically shift from an eternal consciousness to one that is tightly time-locked in the moment. As I also mentioned in the introduction to this book, I can almost imagine them then as puppets of an external consciousness. In this ET-related scenario, while the puppet-master, unseen to the audience, knows the whole play, the puppet does only what it is controlled to do moment-to-moment and, if an audience member were to question the puppet itself, the puppet could only answer from its own limited perspective. The puppet-master itself doesn't answer perhaps because its responses would be something eternal and complex beyond human understanding. These puppet-masters of pure consciousness can't edit down to our narrow level of comprehension and, therefore, we get the puppet's exceptionally finite answer.

So, on the evening the grays brought along a hybrid when visiting me, I think an example of this was on display when I asked them a question and they replied with a confirmation that a question was being asked as their answer.

FINAL THOUGHTS

Many inexplicable things have happened to me for which I have no answers. For this book, I asked myself whether I should I keep to myself those things that I can't explain or should I share everything, regardless of how it sounds?

Many experiencers are understandably somewhat conservative about speaking about their encounters, even with others in the broader UFO community. While some things are shared, there are often additional details that sound too strange, even for those who claim to be sympathetic to the phenomenon.

I did my best here to tell what I could.

Am I saying that there are things that I held back from my accounts in this book, out of concern for the details being too unusual for consumption?

In a way, yes. However, some readers would likely count these items as being ironically both unusual and tedious.

I'm speaking chiefly of synchronicities. Experiencers' lives, myself included, are saturated with these meaningful coincidences. Some examples of how synchronicities play out in my life are the events in the Strange Calls chapter. What I shared there is just the tip of the iceberg. In fact, I could have potentially doubled the length of that chapter alone, but I believe I got some of the bigger synchronicities out of the way without bogging things down. Many more head-scratching coincidences should be evident throughout the book. One could even argue my life has been driven by synchronicities. Oh, and for what it's worth, my numbers are 1111.

In the narrative portion of the book, I state that the events in this volume don't mark the end of the phenomenon for me, so I hope to put out more books, hopefully sooner than a decade-long gap like it's been since my last one.

For the experiencers, please know that there is a vibrant community of individuals out there who have lived lives as imbued as yours who want to meet you. Please go find them.

Should anyone wish to contact me about your experiences, I'm looking forward to meeting you. Cheers.

Experiencer 2

Appendices

Experiencer 2

APPENDIX A. TELEVISION

To any experiencers reading this book, please allow me to address a cautionary topic for your consideration. Should you be brave enough to share your personal encounters with any type of reporters, writers, or media production teams, their capacity to edit your story can sometimes produce substantially inaccurate and, not uncommonly, unfortunately offensive results. Among all of the possible outlets for you to share your accounts, television, in my opinion, is the worst offender.

Over the past twenty years, I've had my share of TV appearances relating my encounters, which has proven to be a mixed bag. This has been a real case of the good, the bad, and the ugly.

With regard to the good, I cannot say enough positive about the 2002 production, *The Abduction Diaries*. The producers were compassionate and detail-oriented, making sure to let us experiencers get our stories told correctly. Kudos to Naked Eyes Productions.

I'm also positive about my interview in the 2014 documentary, *Abducted by Aliens: Encounters of the 4th Kind.* Thank you, Sector 5 Films.

While I am grateful to have had some screen time in *ABC's Peter Jennings: UFOs – Seeing is Believing*, the network made a bad choice by interspersing the interviews of experiencers with the rambling of debunkers, most notably the clumsy efforts of Harvard University's Susan Clancy. It is not a balanced approach to have outsiders to the topic offer personal critiques of something they've never studied scientifically.

There are two examples I have that fall into the ugly category.

In 2011, I was flown by a major cable television network to Roswell, New Mexico, to appear in a UFO documentary. My part, they informed me, was to tell of my encounters in order to give a picture of extraterrestrials are like to go along with what other invited participants were saying about the 1947 crash as well as theories of UFO propulsion.

After interviewing me for several hours inside the Roswell UFO Museum, the documentary's director appeared obviously disconcerted. When I asked him what was wrong, he confessed that the reason they wanted me in the show was to appear a little flaky to add some spice to the production. The problem, he said, was that I came off as too credible and that he believed I was telling the truth (much to his surprise!). I was, therefore, cut completely from the final product.

In another example, in 2012, I was flown to New York City by an independent production studio looking to pitch a show on abductions to the major networks. I agreed that they could interview me for their pilot and, perhaps, hypnotically regress me.

On the day of filming, I met their hypnotist, a nice enough gentleman who had made a name for himself assisting veterans with PTSD. When I asked him about his experience working with abductees, he replied that he had no experience at all and knew next to nothing about the phenomenon. After I confessed to him that this lack of experience made me uncomfortable, he opined that his unfamiliarity with the subject made him more objective and that I shouldn't worry because he'd worked with individuals who were deeply traumatized in other areas for years. This really didn't help much.

So, I was interviewed and then the hypnosis portion began. Whereas I was accustomed to a gentle induction with a prolonged meditative relaxation to begin things, his approach was simply to have me lean forward and uncomfortably rest my forehead on his open palm until he suddenly shoved me back forcefully into the couch while he shouted, "Asleep!" That was it. This was his induction technique.

As I sat startled on the couch, he began asking me on camera to relive an encounter. It should be no surprise that I wasn't remotely regressed. I did my best to recall something for him, but I couldn't concentrate under these conditions and he didn't really know what to do beyond asking me to try harder.

Later, that same afternoon, after the interview and "regression," the producers insisted I go back and redo both and add some drama. Specifically, they asked me to cry. When I told them that I doubted I could do that, my part in their production was effectively over. As I never saw this show on TV, with or without me, I assume they either gave up or no network picked it up.

In these last two situations, I was treated as an actor, not an average individual sharing unusual experiences. The silver lining, at least, to both of these unfortunate episodes is that I got free trips from Detroit to both Roswell and New York City.

Another perk from the New York production was that they arranged to have me take, at no cost, the psychological evaluation known as the Minnesota Multiphasic Personality Index (MMPI PSY 5) prior to them flying me out for filming. The results of the test indicated that I was not fantasy-prone but that I did indicate lingering stress from one or more disturbing events.

As long-time MUFON State Director for Michigan, my television experience has also included a number of appearances on the topic of UFO sightings in my home state. Basically, local news coverage has been a mixed bag and productions for actual UFO shows on major networks have all been ugly. As these experiences not so directly related to the topic of this book, I'll refrain from venting about it all here.

In any case, I'll sum up by saying that the UFO and contact phenomena are textbook examples of "truth is stranger than fiction," but most TV producers apparently take this motto as a dare and work hard to warp true encounters into their own brand of fiction in a misguided effort to jazz them up, benefitting no one. When they're done with the witnesses' encounters, they're neither true nor interesting.

APPENDIX B: BUDD

I felt it appropriate to close with this recollection of my last meeting with the late legendary abduction researcher Budd Hopkins.

Hopkins was a remarkable researcher and a great man. He was warm, funny, personable, and everyone's friend in the UFO community.

By the time I had first met him in the late 1990s at a MUFON Symposium, I had already been competently regressed about the majority of my experiences. So, while I had shared to him some of what had happened to me over the years, he listened compassionately and remarked that I was lucky to have had someone close to me to be able to work through some of the phenomenon's more difficult aspects.

Budd was a regular at these MUFON events, even when he wasn't presenting, and always very approachable. There were many times I was fortunate enough to engage with him over the years.

My very last memory of him is one I'll never forget.

It was at the 2008 MUFON Symposium in San Jose, California, and he and I happened to arrive at the hotel restaurant at the same time on Saturday afternoon, looking for lunch. I asked if he was meeting anyone. He said he wasn't and he asked if I'd like to eat with him. The restaurant was unfortunately quite full, though, and the only available seating was at the bar. Neither of us minded and we sat the bar and chatted while we waited for our meals to arrive. No alcohol for us, just lunch.

The bar itself was one of those that had a central island of liquor surrounded by the bar on four sides. The side opposite of us openly faced outside into a swimming pool area that had sandwich-board signs out, indicating that it was closed to a private event. This event was a social mixer for young adults. When Budd and I first sat to look at our menus, the several bathing-suit clad young men and women outside were fidgeting awkwardly at noticeable distances from one another in the bright sunlight. But, as the liquor flowed for them, things quickly changed outside into an entertaining spectacle.

The young adults started to finally mingle and Budd and I chuckled at one young man who was making the rounds, flexing his muscles and making hooting sounds for some reason. As he started to capture the amused attention of the young women, the other men in the pool area soon realized that they needed to step up their game. One man started singing along to the music quite loudly, while another jogged laps around the outside of the pool, pumping his fists, and two of the men engaged in a fake boxing match.

Things were quickly getting interesting and, by the time our food arrived, Budd and I were enraptured at the show and laughing at their antics.

The two men boxing then started doing aggressive chest bumps with each other, inspiring the two ladies with whom they were speaking to surprisingly also start chest-bumping each-other.

The grand finale was these aforementioned two men in a wheelbarrow race stance, one man in front, walking on his hands, and the other man in back holding up the man in front's legs and walking upright behind him. They waddled ridiculously toward the pool and, as the front man's first hand dipped into the water, they both instantly plummeted in. This was immediately followed by the two women running and screaming in delight right behind them into the water as the two guys resurfaced with big smiles on their faces.

Budd and I were practically in tears, laughing, while no one else inside, likely the majority of them there for the UFO conference, seemed even to notice what was going on outside.

As Budd and I finished our lunch and got up to leave the restaurant, he turned to me and said with a grin, "It's a wonder why they even bother with us."

APPENDIX C: POEMS

This is a collection of poems I wrote about my encounters when I was in my early twenties, during the time-frame of the story. Many correlate to specific encounters from my two books. I make no boast to quality, but they were cathartic exercises putting them to paper.

I've been sleeping in the basement

Slipping through the cosmos

Spiraling complacent

Almost

Almost

❖

With the winds

The curtain drifts

My conscious lifts

And paradigm shifts

I chance a glance outside my shroud

And see lights dance behind a cloud

There are sky truths to be found

Much more to life than what's on ground.

Experiencer 2

One Boy's Winter Curiosity

As the orange sled's journey ends
I roll onto my back
The stars shine in the heavens
But why does one zig-zag ...
That star streaking swiftly northwest
Swerving left and right
Sharply round the rest of them
Then slipping out of sight?

❖

Nothing Natural

Shhh. There's a sound I've never heard
And a feeling too familiar.
For safety's sake,
I must take
Precautions against slumber.

Aloft

Too many times in my teens
I'd awaken to find
A blow to my mind
Unusual scenes
Drifting above
The bed where I slept
Suddenly swept
Up from gravity's glove
Other times waking
In some other room
To begin to assume
Is an undertaking
Out of my bed
And floating the halls
Passing through walls
As if I was dead
This was not by my choice
Not a thing I'd condone
I knew I wasn't alone
Though, for there was a voice (…)

Experiencer 2

One night as I felt
My self separate
And my soul levitate
And reality melt
It bellowed my name
With a cold, bass, ring
I couldn't do anything
And unwillingly came
I can't remember the rest
Of that eerie night
I have no hindsight
But, maybe that's best

❖

buzzticktickticktickhum
creakticktickticktickhum
crackleticktickticktickhum
whooshticktick hush hush

In My Backyard

A summer's night, dimly starred.

I'm in the kitchen. Something's in the backyard.

My senses scream out, "Stand on guard!"

I'm in the kitchen. Someone's in the backyard.

My heart beats heavy, quick, and hard.

I'm in the kitchen. Who's in the backyard?

Childlike creatures, slight and charred.

I'm in the kitchen. They're in the backyard.

They're there in the backyard. In my backyard.

❖

Visit from a Pallid Man

He brings me a book

look, he says, look

I won't take the hook

look look

I'm shaken, I'm shook

look look

look look

look!

Experiencer 2

<u>The Tumbler</u>

An aureate orb

Arcs overhead

Slowly spinning

Shifting Hue

From blue

To white

And then

To red

(What now

Is red

Turned white

From blue).

The Silent Hill

It was a mystery why that trail we followed
That wound through woods that darkness swallowed
Why did we climb that hill that night
And lay our blanket beneath starlight?

It was strange that the summer chorus was hush
The crickets and critters that hide in the bush
The breeze that whips through the trees was still
As she and I stargazed upon the hill

It was queer how we peered up oblivious
To the surreal stillness surrounding us
Our warm skin showered with thick insect spray
But it couldnt keep their kind away

What happened next, we can't quite explain
On the hill at the end of the dusty lane
We weren't alone, of that we were sure
Bug men! But the rest, we just wonder

Experiencer 2

<u>Charred Gray (song lyrics)</u>

Some wonder why I sleep by day.
At night, I shun my pillow.
I'm plagued by creatures of charred gray
And ,where they come from, I don't know.
At night they come to take me away
(don't want to leave, don't want to go),
But even if I beg to stay,
Does it matter?
No.
No.
No.

How can you preach and bang your drum
And try to tell me where they're from?

How can you tell me that they care?
To put it plainly, you weren't there.

<u>Angel</u>

I was very alone

Seems I'm always alone

When they come to me

In their silent tone

The three little men

Had brought me a friend

Why they did, I'm not sure

I felt so sorry for her

It was very dark

Seems it's always dark

When they come to me

Cold and stark

She was thin and pale

Sallow and stale

I named her Angel

And they bid me farewell

It was very late

Seems it's always late

When they come to me

In my weary state

Experiencer 2

Me & You

You bestow me

You rob me

You watch me

You ignore me

You protect me

You cut me

You soothe me

You frighten me

You energize me

You exhaust me

You enlighten me

You confuse me

You take me

You deliver me

You know me

Revolve

If you don't tell me,

I won't make it easy.

I won't go along

If I don't know from wrong.

As I tread into tomorrow,

From been, through am, to be,

I will always turn it inside-out

And raise the mercury.

Experiencer 2

<u>Nocturnauts</u>

When I was young

I saw the sun

As firewall and friend.

Allied against the nocturnauts

Interloping know-not-whats

Who'd come calling at days end.

Until the daunters said don't fear

For faithfully they would be here

Often by bedside.

That from my future's whence they hail

And their passings in moonlight pale

Hadn't harmed me 'til I died.

And even as I entered death

Years from now, my final breath

Eased me into common ground

The nocturnauts and I had found.

Hinterland

As I walked past the dead trees
And evergreens of winter breeze

The homes had dimmed their glow

As I walked along the frozen lake
And brushed away collecting flakes

Of softly blowing snow

I passed a modest house of gray
With a man so strange in the driveway

A charcoal skinned and white-eyed being
Small but peering and all-seeing

He spoke to me inside my mind
And warned me that the road would wind

"Your path shall snake, so know your friends
From highwaymen as the road bends"

Experiencer 2

I was floating through

Eyes cerulean blue

And now that I'm on true confessions

I miss you

❖

<u>To my Friends</u>

On a Saturday at someone's home

Or by email or telephone

My friends and I will work things out

We'll work it out, together.

The victims of abuse and

The explorers free to choose

My friends and I

We'll work things out

Will work it out, together.

SOURCES

Books

Baum, L. Frank. *The Wonderful Wizard of Oz*. George M. Hill, 1900.

Jacobs, David Phd. *Secret Life: Firsthand Documented Accounts of UFO Abductions*. Fireside, 1992.

Konkolesky, William. *Experiencer: Raised in Two Worlds*. Lulu, 2009.

Television & Film

Abducted by Aliens: Encounters of the 4th Kind. Directed by J Michael Long, Sector 5 films, 2014.

Abduction Diaries. Directed by Jane C. Wagner and Tina Difeliciantonio, Naked Eyes Productions, 2002.

Peter Jennings Reporting: UFOs - Seeing is Believing. Produced by Mark Obenhaus and Tom Yellin, ABC News, 2005.

Music

A House. *I Want Too Much*, Sire, 1990.

Organizations

Center for UFO Studies. *cufos.org*

Michigan Mutual UFO Network. *mimufon.org*

Mutual UFO Network. *mufon.com*

Thank you for reading *Experiencer 2: Two Worlds Collide*

Bill Konkolesky

experiencer.me

beyond

cosmic

Beyond Cosmic Productions

Experiencer 2

CPSIA information can be obtained
at www.ICGtesting.com
Printed in the USA
LVHW051600090322
712905LV00015B/1276

9 781716 464324